Guiding Your
Catholic
Preschooler

Kathy Pierce
&
Lori Rowland

Our Sunday Visitor Publishing Division
Our Sunday Visitor, Inc.
Huntington, Indiana 46750

Our Sunday Visitor Publishing Division
Our Sunday Visitor, Inc.
200 Noll Plaza
Huntington, IN 46750

ISBN: 0-87973-392-6
LCCCN: 2001-131193

Cover design by Monica Haneline
Interior design by Sherri L. Hoffman

PRINTED IN THE UNITED STATES OF AMERICA

To Our Lady,
the Blessed Mother of us all,
without whom this book would
never have been written.

TABLE OF CONTENTS

ACKNOWLEDGMENTS

My first thanks go to my mom and dad, Leitner and Ken Greiner. Wow! How do you thank your parents? First, they taught me the Catholic faith . . . so few words for so much meaning! They opened the gates of eternal life to my family and me. More recently, if it weren't for them, this book would still be in rough draft. For the hours of reading, editing, typing, daughter-prodding, prayerful and financial support, and baby-sitting while I worked — thank you.

Thank you, Larry, my husband, for being my best friend. It must have been difficult living with a pregnant lady who was writing a book.

And a thank you to my children — Bretton, Wade, Leigha, Marianne, Julia Grace, and John Paul — for the opportunity to share the Catholic faith. They are so eager to learn, so anxious to know about God — if only we could imitate their enthusiasm. Their beautiful gift of faith and their constant reminding will hopefully be the means of my salvation!

A special thank you to Lori and Paul Rowland, two of my very best friends in Christ. There are several chapters to their credit, as well as countless hours of editing and proofing. I'm sure I couldn't have added the section on the Internet on my own. And it was Lori who helped me realize years ago that I was not alone in trying not only to teach but also to help my children *live* their faith. She promised me that I wasn't "too overprotective, too religious or fanatical" and all the other adjectives I've been called.

Thank you to my brother, Don Greiner, and his wife, Shellie. Their addition of the sections on "Witnessing the Love of Christ to Your Preschooler" and "Memorizing Basic prayers and Scripture" are God-inspired. They are true examples of Christlike Catholic parents. Their ability and willingness to share the wisdom and knowledge that God has bestowed upon them touch and impact the lives of all who know them, know their children, or read their input in this book.

I want to thank Bill Whitmore and his wife, Therese, for their many years of work. Also, thank you to the teams at Good Catholic Books, the Mary Foundation, and Saint Jude Media.

The help of Mary Jo Ogle, Jeanne (Kirby) Gorman, Linda Bauman, and Vonda Smith is much appreciated — thank you!

Finally, and most importantly, a glorious, honorable, well-deserved, best-thanks-ever to Mother Mary for being there for me from the beginning and continuing my journey with me every day. She has often enveloped me in her mantle. Without her guidance, help, support, prayers, and love, I would be more distant from her Son. In desperately fleeing to her Immaculate Heart, I hope to come to the presence of His Most Sacred Heart. I hope that, through its fruits, my work can be pleasing to her and her Son. I want more than anything for my children and all people to be with her one day.

— KATHY PIERCE

foreword

Train up a child in the way he should go, and when he is old he will not depart from it. — PROVERBS 22:6

PASS ON THE FAITH

In an age of alluring toys and beeping technology, it is encouraging to see young parents experiencing the joy of parenthood and passing on the spiritual truths and practices of the Catholic faith to their family in the early formative years.

Kathy Pierce, a mother of six children under the age of 14, and her husband, Larry, are loving parents. Years ago, as one of my parishioners, she was very involved in parish life, and she remains active in the Church today. Among other things, she has taught Vacation Bible School and religion classes for the pre-K toddlers.

Lori Rowland and her husband, Paul, are raising four children under the age of 13. They are active in St. Joseph Parish, Jacksonville, Florida.

Kathy found Catholic material for older children, but very little for small folk. The practical day-to-day suggestions for faith-development of Catholic children came from combined ideas and practices that she and Lori have set down in this book, with the hope that since these things worked for them, others might find them helpful.

To teach one to see beyond the external comes from a persistent spiritual frame of reference. It builds on inherited tendencies and redirects behavioral patterns. Kathy makes spiritual things fun and has "simplified" the mysteries of the Catholic faith in a way that toddlers can assimilate at their level and love doing it. I think this book not only offers hundreds of helps but also basically confirms that children are intrinsically religious, if only the opportunities are offered. At an early age, they can appreciate sacred space (the house of God), time (seasons), and people (saints). Her frequent ear-whispering at daily Mass must make attentiveness at Sunday Mass easier. The ground rules have already been set.

I heartily congratulate Kathy for sharing her experiences and efforts with all her readers.

— REV. JOHN MICHALICKA
Pastor
Church of St. Mary
Ponca City, Oklahoma

introduction

Like arrows in the hand of a warrior are the sons of one's youth. Happy is the man who has his quiver full of them! — PSALM 127:4-5

A JOYFUL RESPONSIBILITY

A young child's mind is ready to absorb, process, and retain an enormous quantity of information! As parents, you watch your child discover a vast scope of secular information about the world around him every day. A child can begin learning about the rich tradition and ritual of the Catholic faith as well.

Many Catholic churches do not begin formal weekly religious education until a child is 4 or 5 years old. Parents teach a child a wealth of information about the world around him and how to live in society long before the first day of any parish catechism class. Parents teach every day. They should accept the joyful responsibility of teaching the Catholic faith, too.

Do not expect priests and religious-education teachers to carry the burden of teaching all there is about the Catholic faith. Strive every day to keep the commitment you made when you had your child baptized. Realize and appreciate your vocation of motherhood and fatherhood. Fulfilling your responsibility will take time and effort. God will reward you abundantly!

The Primary Goal of Every Parent

Your primary goal should be to attain eternal salvation for yourself and your family. To do this, you must love and serve God and guide your children to do the same. Developing a loving relationship with Mary, Our Blessed Mother, will help you. After all, her mission is to bring all souls to her Son. Through such a strong personal relationship, your child's love for God and Mary will be everlasting. When he gets older and is challenged in his faith, it will be difficult and perhaps impossible for your child to abandon the relationship that you have instilled between him and the Church, the saints (including the Blessed Virgin Mary), and the Triune God.

Any relationship takes time and effort to develop. This is true whether it be family, a friend, or God. Help your child to know God so that he can love Him. You may find that your own knowledge of God is lacking — and in the process of teaching your child about God, you may find yourself coming to a deeper knowledge of Him at the same time.

You cannot love someone you do not know! The more you and your child put into this friendship, the more you both will gain from it.

Mary can become a best friend and a true mother. She is an advocate. She can go to God and ask a favor. Developing a relationship with her will bring you and your child closer to Jesus, her Son, and to the Holy Spirit, her spouse. Her mission has always been to point you to Jesus and bring you to God. Have recourse to her, and you and your child will come to a deeper knowledge of God, which in turn will translate into a deep and abiding sense of the presence and love of God.

Consecration

Consecrate, or dedicate, your home, your life, your family, and your day to the Sacred Heart of Jesus and the Immaculate Heart of Mary. Ask Jesus daily to be the King of your family. Recite daily, "Most Sacred Heart of Jesus, I put my trust in You." Appendix II contains two beautiful consecration prayers that both you and your child can recite each morning.

Set an Example —
"Lay down your life for your children . . ."

A child learns by example. He will imitate you. He will imitate the way you act, eat, dress, and worship. Therefore, it is essential that you set a good example by *your* life. What is important to you will be important to him.

You cannot bring others, including your children, to holiness unless you continually strive for holiness yourself. Foster a personal relationship with Christ in the sacraments. It is an endless and awesome journey. Always continue to grow in your faith and love for God.

Let your child see and hear you happily exercise your faith in your daily life. Set personal goals for yourself, such as resolving to: attend daily Mass or to make a Spiritual Communion if you are unable to attend daily Mass; receive the Sacrament of Reconciliation regularly; make a Morning Offering to God; read the daily Mass readings from the Bible; make a Holy Hour of Adoration once a week; greet Mary in the afternoons with the Angelus; pray a mystery of the Rosary daily; deny yourself with fasting. At the end of the day, examine your conscience and make an Act of Contrition.

Integrate your faith with your life. Set guidelines and stick to them. For example, since you must attend Mass on Sunday, be sure you attend Mass even if you are out of town or on vacation. How awesome it is to know and see that in whatever city or country you are in, the Catholic Liturgy of the Word and Eucharist will be celebrated in the same basic way!

Give meaning and excitement to what you do with your religion. Your values will be transmitted to your child. Always continue to grow and learn in your faith. Read books, watch educational videos, attend retreats. Make time to develop your own relationship with your Creator in the same way you want your child to grow in his relationship with you. Be a *good* example.

Modesty

Modesty in dress is extremely important. Set a good example! Our body is *not* to be a near occasion of sin for others but rather a temple of the Holy Spirit, and we should adorn it as such! Unfortunately in our society, this presents a challenge for mothers of children of all ages. You must be alert and open to see the disgrace in what we may have become desensitized toward. *It's okay to be offended when you see something inappropriate — and to tell your kids so!* You must also be prepared to work a little harder than most people to spend time shopping.

Appropriate clothing should be an issue with both boys and girls, and it should be evaluated in church clothes, swim suits, and daily wear.

Clothing *will* present challenges as your children get older. Insist that they grow up with *extreme* modesty. Then, even when you "give in" at some point, the results will hopefully still be modest. If you do have a question or concern, or if your children argue with you, ask yourself, and them, these questions: (1) Would Mother Mary (or Jesus) wear that, even today? (2) Would you feel comfortable in those clothes, at this activity, with Mother Mary *and* Jesus at your side? (They are always with us!)

Working Mothers/Single Parents

Although this book was written by two mothers who stay at home, both worked for several years while their children attended day care. Just as cooking and cleaning are difficult to fit into your schedule, so is religious education. However, teaching your faith is still essential and very possible. Make time to teach your child about God. Do not let a secular world interfere with your primary responsibility and joy as a Catholic parent!

More Than One Child

It's important to talk to each child at his own level. What you point out and explain to your 2-year-old during Mass will be much more simple and tangible than what you teach your 4-year-old. The questions that come from each will be different, too! Do not feel bad if you cannot answer a question. Make a promise to take the time to research the answer, and then keep your promise.

Pray with each child. Talk about God with each of them every day. Avoid focusing on one child, causing another to receive less attention. Finally, resist getting tired or bored with teaching religion to the last child in line. He is just as eager and willing to learn as the first!

When to Start

Start when your child is born. If you have missed this moment, start now! There are many ideas included in this book that you can use from day one, and it's never too late to begin! Lay the foundation early for further education. He's so eager to learn when he's very young, and he trusts and believes all you teach him. Take advantage of it!

Be alert for good opportunities to teach. When you read a religious book or article, mention it to your child. Throughout your day, watch for good things to be thankful for. Integrate prayer and God into every action, including meals, bedtime, discipline, and the host of activities and experiences you have each day. This book will help you get started. You're sure to develop and implement many more ideas as you and your child's relationship with God grows.

Where to Start

First, teach your child about God — the Father, the Son, and the Holy Spirit — and Mary. They are real. They know and love your child. Do not suggest to your child that "some people do not believe in God" or "some people do not think Jesus is God." Young children shouldn't doubt. They shouldn't be introduced to the dissension that has occurred in the Church. They should trust and believe what you tell them! As they get older, they will be exposed to other religions and, sadly, "controversial" issues in their own faith. At that time, you can explain and have long conversations with them regarding the *Catechism of the Catholic Church* and papal encyclicals. You can explain that often some people don't fully understand Jesus and His teachings. We must not judge these people, but we must pray for them.

Teach your child about Old and New Testament characters. Teach him that these were real people, with real-life faith and love of God! Protestant parents introduce very young children to these characters. Yet some Catholics shy away from teaching the Bible to their children. We may even tend to become judgmental of those who sometimes seem so knowledgeable. Don't be afraid or hesitant! Learn by doing and reading! Learn with your child. Pray with your child. Open yourself to grow in your relationship with God as you teach your child.

Include the saints. They're special friends of God. Their lives reflect God's love. They are good examples for us. As you learn and teach about them, they'll become your friends.

Daddy Is Important

Mothers, pray for your child's father. Pray that he understands and appreciates the importance of his role in his child's life.

Mothers, praise Dad's involvement with his child: "Honey, I like the way you explained to Tommy how trains work"; "Dear, you're very good with Annie and her baby dolls"; or "You are very patient with John and I appreciate it." Brag about Dad. Let Dad know he is valuable and appreciated. This will encourage him to increase his contact with his child.

Many daddies do not believe that their role is important to their child's early development. Nothing could be further from the truth.

Dad, realize that your example is important to your pre-school child. Participate with your child in his play, work, sports, education, and prayer. The rewards will be limitless!

Daddies, become involved in your child's religious education, too. Take your child to Mass. Help him make the Sign of the Cross. Encourage good behavior at church. Read Bible and saint stories to him. Let your child see and hear you pray.

Use St. Joseph as your example. St. Joseph was a good Jewish father. He went to the synagogue every week and celebrated all the holy days and traditions. He passed these down to Jesus. He was a good provider and teacher. He was a hardworking carpenter, and he taught Jesus his trade. St. Joseph was also a good spouse to Mary. He was protective and gentle, loving and firm. He was a prayerful man, with his mind always open and obedient to the will of God.

St. Joseph was a man of action. When he felt God leading and directing him, he acted. In the middle of the night, when asked to go to Egypt, he wasted no time in responding.

Ask St. Joseph to guide you in your vocation as a father. Ask him to pray with you to the Father, that you may imitate him in his role as the foster-father of Jesus.

Your Friends

Choose adult friends with whom you share the same values and priorities. Encourage playtime and friendships between their child and yours. Do not be afraid or ashamed to teach your child religion. Use religion as you lovingly discipline your child while you are with these friends. Jesus said that following Him would not always be easy.

Situations will arise when you have to decide between your faith and peer pressure from friends. For example, what movie or video is "everyone" seeing? Do you feel it is appropriate for your child?

What about telling a "white lie" that your child overhears? The saints teach us that there are ramifications for even the smallest lie: It perpetuates itself. Do you tell a ticket seller that your child is younger than he is so that you can get a cheaper entry fee? Everyone else is doing it! Be prepared for these situations. Be determined when the time comes to face these issues.

If your friends become critical, non-supportive, or disrespectful of you and your decisions, you must evaluate the quality and importance of your friendship. You must also evaluate why they feel the way they do, but never be judgmental of them.

Always put God first, your family next, and everything else after that. These are your priorities!

Your Home

In your home, visual reminders of the most important people in your life are valuable, for children and adults. When you see a family photograph taken long ago, it triggers memories and thoughts. This is also true of religious articles. You don't "worship idols," but the images can encourage special thoughts and prayers throughout each day.

For the sake of you and your child's spiritual growth, include reminders of your faith as well. Make crucifixes, pictures, books, and statues visible. (There are more ideas in Chapter 4.) You may find your home becoming filled with religious items, books, and other signs of your faith. Do what is comfortable for you and your family.

In your home, practice your faith in the way that you feel is best. Do what is necessary for you and your family to steadfastly grow in your faith and devotion. Do not be concerned with the opinion of your friends. Your God, and your family, come first. If your example affects your friends and their children, praise God!

Answering Your Child's Questions

A child has lots of questions about the world around him. The more things he is exposed to, the more questions he will ask. If you take him to the zoo, he will ask about animals. If you go to a sporting event, questions will come up about the game. If you take him to church, he will ask about God. If you read the Bible to him and teach him about Jesus, God, and Mary, questions will be abundant on these subjects, too. This is only natural, as the child wants to know and understand everything. Be thankful that he turns to you and asks questions, rather than keeping it all inside and wondering. It could be worse. He may ask his less knowledgeable little friends!

But how do you answer these often difficult, but very good questions? First of all, do not panic. Instead, say a silent, quick prayer like, "Dear God, please help me with this one!" Try not to *over*-answer a question. Keep your answer simple and brief. Your answer does not have to be profound. Satisfy his curiosity while teaching him about his faith.

After answering the question, ask your child if he understands: "Does that sound like a good answer to you?" If he is confused or does not understand, repeat your answer, or repeat it with different words. Be patient, even if you must answer the question several times!

If you really cannot come up with an answer, tell your child you do not know: "When we get home, we'll look it up in the Bible" or "Let's go by the church and see if Father is there, and maybe he can help us." Of course, these are less desirable because an hour later the issue will not be nearly as important to your child as it was when asked.

The questions will be endless. A question may be easy or difficult, but it is always a serious and important matter to your child. Do your best to answer it as such. Keep it simple!

Using This Book

This book contains several specific ideas to help you get started immediately. Many are short and simple. Some will require a little preparation on your part. Some you will probably question as to whether or not they are appropriate for your child.

Do not try to implement all of these suggestions simultaneously. Select an idea that appeals to you. Then set a goal for your child and for you. As you reach one goal, add another. For example, start reading a children's Bible once a day to your child. Next month work on the Sign of the Cross, while continuing to read the Bible. Allow your child the opportunity to grow in his spiritual knowledge!

Remember, every little success contributes to the child's overall vision of his faith. Any progress, no matter how small it may seem, will be better than the alternative. God will be pleased. Never will your efforts be in vain. Always your efforts will be rewarded!

Ask God to Help You

Pray for guidance. God will help you teach your child. He will guide you if you ask Him. After all, no one knows your child better than you and God!

chapter one

First of all, then, I urge that supplications, prayers, intercessions, and thanksgivings be made for all men. . . . This is good, and it is acceptable in the sight of God our Savior, who desires all men to be saved and to come to the knowledge of the truth.

— 1 TIMOTHY 2:1, 3-4

PRAYER

Teach Your Child to Pray

Praying is communicating with God and should be part of your way of life. It is not a separate activity for special occasions. Praying every day is vital for you and your child. Teaching your child to pray every day helps him develop a relationship with God. It is your most important responsibility as a parent.

Set a good example of a prayerful life. Set aside quiet time for your own personal prayers. Your child can join you, but these are your prayers. There is no better teacher than good example by a parent. Do not allow prayer to become monotonous and boring. If your child is restless, change your pattern of prayer. You do not want prayer to become a dreaded chore.

What a blessing it is if you can begin when the child is in the womb. He hears and feels your thoughts and prayers before birth. Continue when your child is born and still an infant. The more you pray with him, formally and informally, the more spontaneous and natural prayer will be in his life.

Over the years, the important relationship with God the Father, the Son, and the Holy Spirit will be formed and developed through prayer. A stable, strong foundation will be built. As the child grows, he may challenge this friendship with God, experiencing good times and bad. However, the stronger the foundation and the more time and effort given in prayer to developing an intensive love and incredible faith, the more the friendship will be affirmed.

God will be there for your child. Encourage him always to turn to God every day, and he'll learn to do it on his own! Prayer will become his way of life.

When to Pray

Pray in the morning and in the evening. Pray at naptime and playtime. Pray on a walk, in the car, when you hear a siren, and when you eat a meal. Pray when something special or good happens to you or your family, or in time of sorrow. Pray in time of need. Say prayers of thanksgiving. Pray formally and informally. Pray many exclamatory prayers (found in this chapter). Pray any time you think of it. Pray often.

Develop this habit early. This is so important! A child as young as age 1 will love to "pray" with you. You may find that at times your mind becomes preoccupied and you forget to pray. Your preschooler will remind you to pray! He may become the means to your salvation!

Pray as a Family

Include your entire family together in prayer daily. This can be mealtime, drive time, bedtime, or after dinner before watching television or playing with toys.

Mention why you're praying: "It makes God happy when we talk to Him. He is so good to us and is so special. It's important we talk with Him every day! Let's see, what special things shall we pray for today?"

This can lead to a moment of silence before prayer. This quiet time will open your hearts to God and will help create a special relationship with Him that cannot be achieved any other way. Prayer is a rich family tradition and will certainly change and grow as your child gets older. For example, you could develop the habit of praying a daily Rosary together as a family.

Holy Is His Name!

Teach your child that the name of Jesus is special and holy. St. Paul says, "At the name of Jesus, every knee should bow, in heaven and on earth and under the earth, and every tongue confess that Jesus Christ is Lord" (Philippians 2:10-11).

A beautiful tradition in the Church that seems to be lost in this country is the bowing of heads at the name of Jesus. You may look around during a church Rosary and see the heads of older gentlemen and ladies bow during each Hail Mary when they arrive at the words "blessed is the fruit of thy womb, *Jesus.*"

The name of Jesus is powerful. He can forgive, heal, cast out devils, give life in baptism, and give eternal salvation. Our culture has a tendency to depict Jesus as our friend and buddy. Do not lose sight of the fact that He is our Lord and our God! Teach your child deep reverence for His Holy Name.

Exclamatory Prayers

These short, simple prayers can be fun and powerful. They are easy to learn. Try and make them a habit throughout your day. Suggestions include:

- Praise God!
- Thank God!
- Jesus and Mary, I love You! Save souls!
- Lord Jesus Christ, Son of God, have mercy on me a sinner!
- Lord, have mercy!
- Let it be done to me according to Thy word!
- Thy will be done!
- Come, Holy Spirit!
- Forgive them, Lord, they know not what they do!
- God bless Father _____ (our priest)!

You can get many more ideas from Sacred Scripture and the writings of the saints.

Learning the Sign of the Cross

In our Catholic tradition, the Sign of the Cross is one of our oldest prayers. It dates back to the early Christians, and perhaps to the apostles. We honor and glorify the name of God with the Sign of the Cross. Crossing ourselves can be how we say "Hello" and "Good-bye" to God when we talk to Him in formal prayer. We're inviting Him to be with us. When we trace a cross on our body, we are also shielding ourselves against evil.

Children love to color, outline, and trace. When we make the Sign of the Cross, we are "tracing" God's love for us. We're asking the three Persons of the Trinity to envelop us! It's important that your child learn this early. He'll learn to do this by watching and imitating you.

A helpful trick in teaching the Sign of the Cross is to use your left hand instead of the right, and to touch your right shoulder first instead of the correct left. Your child will copy you, but in doing so he will being doing it the correct way. He'll stare at you and imitate your hand movement. He'll look like your mirror image.

As an alternative, have the child sit beside you while looking in the mirror. Have him copy your movements. He'll then be doing it correctly.

Allowing your child to make these movements on his own will make a stronger impression than your holding his right hand, guiding his movements, and then having him repeat from memory. Slowly say the words, "In the name of the Father, and of the Son, and of the Holy Spirit. Amen," as you cross yourself. Over time, your child will begin to repeat you, and then finally say it with you.

Don't be strict and impatient if he makes a mistake. You don't want to frustrate him. Instead, praise his efforts. He's trying! He's proud of himself! He's learning!

Morning Prayer

You should pray every morning before you ever see your child. When you open your eyes, turn your thoughts to God. There are several nice, short prayers you can say, including the Morning Offering, the Daily Consecration to the Sacred and Immaculate Hearts of Jesus and Mary, and the Lord's Prayer. Simple pleas such as St. Francis of Assisi's motto, "All for You, Lord," and others such as "Lord, help me live in Your Divine Will today" and "Mary, be my guide" are also wonderful.

Having a crucifix near your bed is an excellent way to remind yourself upon awakening of how much God loves your family. You may want to kiss the cross as a morning ritual as you make an offering of your day.

In addition, keep a candle on your kitchen table. Light the candle, say your prayer, and then allow the child to blow out the candle. In fact, if you have more than one child, you may have to re-light it for each child to blow out — or collect more candles! Perhaps a mealtime habit will be formed.

The candle is important because it helps keep the child's attention. Also, you can tell the child that Jesus is like the light of the candle. Jesus is the Light of the world! He's bright and makes people feel happy.

The child must complete his prayers before he blows out the candle:

1. Make the Sign of the Cross.
2. Hold his hands in prayer.
3. Say the same prayer every day. Repetition is important to assist in memorizing the prayer. A good prayer is this:

    O Jesus,
    I give You today,
    all that I think
    and do and say. Amen.

    After he learns this prayer, you can expand it:

    Dear God and Mary,
    Please help me today
    with all that I think
    and do and say. Amen.

    Another good prayer is to your guardian angel, which can be found in Chapter 4. A 2-year-old can memorize these prayers.

4. Make the Sign of the Cross again.
5. Then he can blow out the candle!

If you forget to pray at breakfast, say a prayer anytime that you remember to do it. Driving in the car or dressing your child are good times to offer the day to God.

Adoration of Jesus in the Blessed Sacrament

Adoring Jesus exposed in the monstrance is awesome. This is the best place to ask for help! Some parishes provide Perpetual Adoration, while others have it on certain days or times. If your parish does not offer this opportunity, visit the Blessed Sacrament reserved in the tabernacle.

Set a time that you can go alone, without your child. If you, as a parent, could spend one hour each week with Jesus in quiet solitude, He will bless you abundantly as your personal relationship with Him deepens. Do not deny yourself this prayer time! Not only will it be life-changing for your family, but you will also be setting a good example of prayer for your child.

When your child is an infant, he can go with you and stay an hour. As he gets older, you may find his ability to remain still and quiet more challenging. However, you can still "stop in" for a visit to Jesus, even if you stay only a few minutes. This should be in addition to your hour of solitude. Take a rosary, or hold holy cards or a Bible for your child — and be thankful for fifteen minutes! This can be the beginning of a lifelong commitment to Christ.

Praying the Rosary

The Rosary is a gift from Mary. It's a tool for us to contemplate the New Testament, specifically the mysteries of Our Lord. Mary asks us to pray the Rosary. She wants us to come closer to her Son by meditating on His life, death, resurrection, and glorification. It can become one of the most meaningful avenues for contemplative prayer, the most intimate form of prayer. With the exception of the Holy Eucharist and Sacred Scripture, it is the deepest form of communion we can have with God.

Your relationship with the Blessed Mother and her Son will only blossom as your devotion and commitment to the Holy Rosary grows. Do not deprive your child of developing such an awesome, inspiring, and incomprehensibly beautiful relationship with God and Our Lady.

"I Don't Know the Rosary. How Can I Set an Example?"

Learn by doing! There are countless books, holy cards, and tapes available that will guide you through the actual prayers and mysteries of the Rosary. Many will teach you the "fruits" of the mysteries as well. Have one of these books or cards with you as you say the prayers.

At first, the Rosary may seem monotonous. You may feel your mind wandering. Do not give up! Bring your heart back to your prayers (see Appendix I).

When you have accomplished this, you can pray the Rosary anytime throughout your day without a lot of concentration on "what comes next." At times, you may need to listen to God. This could become contemplative prayer, a time when Our Lord and Our Lady will speak to you in a quiet way. Open your heart and let them in!

Your Child and the Rosary

Allow your child frequent access to a rosary. Let him see your rosary next to your bed, in your purse or pocket, or perhaps in the car. Keep one near his bed and within his reach. Let him touch it and hold it. Let him know it is special — no throwing, swinging, or hitting with it. If that happens, you should take it away! Be even more protective if the rosary has been blessed.

Buy him his own rosary. This can be very inexpensive and safe. For young children, ages 1 to 3, find one made of string and plastic beads or of knotted cord. Avoid the small chain-link rosaries. These can break, be swallowed, or scratch sensitive skin. As your child gets older, he can be given more responsibility to carefully care for his own rosary.

Arrange for your child to hear the Rosary being prayed on a regular basis. This can be done in several ways:

1. Say it yourself, in a low whisper, in the child's room, after you have said his nightly prayers with him. He can hold his own rosary while he listens to you and as he falls asleep. He will fall asleep in prayer!

2. Go to Mass fifteen to twenty minutes early with your child. Say the Rosary together before the Blessed Sacrament. Your child will play on the seat and climb over your legs, but he is hearing and subconsciously absorbing the prayers.

3. Pray the Rosary as a family at home. Turn off the television, go to your room, unplug the phone, kneel, and take a few minutes to pray together. Your child can hold his own rosary and "pray" with it while the older family members pray. As your child grows up, he will look back on these special family prayerful times with fond memories.

4. Say the Rosary on car trips, even short trips. Let him hear it being said while traveling.

5. Say only a decade of the Rosary with him on occasion, especially if time does not allow the entire Rosary. This is brief, but nice.

6. Find a book with pictures depicting each mystery. As you pray the Rosary, allow your child to hold and display to your family the picture of the mystery you are contemplating.

7. As your children get older, allow them to lead decades of the Rosary. They will take great pride in active participation.

Bedtime Prayers

Always, always end the day in prayer. You should pray even if the child only listens, or even if he is not listening! Never force him to repeat after you. Expect his participation to be better some nights than others. He may get on his knees very reverently with his hands folded and repeat after you word for word, or he may lie down and fall asleep in the middle of the Lord's Prayer.

He's little, and he learns by example. If you force him to repeat prayers, it could lead to resentment and negative feelings about prayer. Continue to close every day with prayer.

After making the Sign of the Cross, pray the Lord's Prayer, the Hail Mary, and the Glory Be. If your child is really very tired, say only these prayers, but always say these three. If he is not so tired, add spontaneous prayers.

Pray as many spontaneous prayers as your family would like. Ask for blessings for your immediate family, for priests, and for others that your child knows. You can add prayers of thanksgiving for things you did or gifts received from God throughout the day. You can thank God for the rain or sun, for "my bed" — or for that great lunch his friend's mom made for him!

You can add "help me learn" prayers relating to situations your child encountered that day: "Help me learn to share my toys, to be nice to my friends, not to hit my brother anymore, to mind Mom and Dad"; "I'm sorry for jumping on the furniture" or "for push-ing (or hitting) my friend. I will really try to do better."

Add "take care" prayers and begin helping him realize how fortunate and blessed he is: "Take care of kids who don't have mommies or daddies. Take care of people who are cold tonight because they don't have a house to keep them warm, and take care of people who are hungry."

This may seem like a strange thing to pray for with a young child. He may not really understand what you are saying. As he gets a little older, he will ask about these people. It will allow you to teach him about almsgiving, and about giving of clothes and food to the poor. Be sensitive to the emotional level of your child on praying for these issues. You do not want to worry, depress, or scare your child. Keep it as light as possible. As he gets older, pray for resolutions of specific situations that occur in his life or in the world. (Be careful not to do this when he is very young.)

Bedtime is also a good time to memorize new prayers, such as the Act of Contrition, the Apostles' Creed, the Hail Holy Queen, the Memorare of St. Bernard, and the Prayer to the Holy Spirit. If you don't know the prayers, find a prayer card or book with the prayer and begin reading it nightly. Learn the prayers *with* your child!

End your prayers by saying, "I love You, God. I love You, Jesus. I love you, Mary. Amen." This is simple and your child will soon be able to say it with you. It is a definitive ending. He knows you are finished praying. Finally, it is a good, posi-tive, happy prayer in and of itself.

Close by making the Sign of the Cross.

When you kiss your child good night, say, "I love you and God loves you, too, because you are *so* special. And you love God, too! He made you a special kid, you know." Say this to him frequently.

Also, bless your child as you close your prayers: "Dear God, bless little John. Help him sleep well, think of You, and love You his whole life. Amen." As you say this, trace the Sign of the Cross on his forehead. This may also help comfort him as he falls asleep.

Scared at Night

It is common for a child to be frightened at night. Every parent deals with this differently. You might suggest that the child say a prayer asking God or his guardian angel for help (see the Guardian Angel Prayer in Chapter Four or Appendix II). A conversation might go like this:

"Mommy, I'm scared."

"Why? What's wrong?"

"I don't know. It's dark and someone is going to get me."

"Did you say a prayer?"

"No."

"Let's say a prayer: 'Dear God, please help me not be scared. Make whatever is scaring me go away. Thank you for a great day, and help me have a great day tomorrow, too. Help me have fun when I go to my friend's house and play with their puppy. Thank you for taking care of me. Help me sleep well tonight. I love You, Jesus. I love You, God. I love you, Mary. Amen.' Okay, God will help you sleep a little better. I love you and God really loves you very much. Good night."

You will be surprised at how much you put your child at ease. You have changed his thoughts from fear to anticipation for tomorrow. And since you asked, God will help the child sleep. He will "take away" whatever was scaring your child. If a child is scared, it is not of God; in the name of God, any unclean spirit who scares your child is powerless!

Pray Throughout Your Day

Stimulate your child to think about God continually, recognizing Him in all you do throughout your day. This can be used in disciplining, thanksgiving, and interacting with other children. You can bring Him into conversation while driving down the road, going on a walk, or playing in the house. A few sample suggestions follow:

1. *Discipline.* Discipline and punishment, unfortunately, are necessary at times. However, you can turn these unhappy moments into opportunities for teaching your child about God, His love, and His forgiveness: "You shouldn't push or hit other children. That does not make God happy"; "When you hit your friend, it hurts God because he's God's buddy, just like you"; or "Tonight in our prayers, we'll tell God we're sorry for making up a story that's not true, because God knows what really happened and He doesn't like us to tell a lie."

2. *Thanksgiving.* "Thank you, God, for that great tree and letting me climb it"; "Thank you, God, for my friend"; or "Thank you, God, for letting me help my mom and dad today, because I know it makes them so happy."

3. *Interacting With Other Children.* "Dear God, help me share my toys"; "Thank you, God, for letting my friend come over to play"; or "Help me, God, to learn to play nicely with my friend."

4. *Driving Down the Road.* "Thank you, God, for making these 'happy clouds' and not 'rain clouds' today so we can go to the park." On hearing a siren or seeing an emergency vehicle: "Someone needs help and the fire truck is going to help. Oh, dear God, please help those people

who are hurt or need help, Please help the workers and doctors take care of the sick person. Thy will be done!" You could also pray, "Dear God, please help Grandma feel better because she's sick today" or "There's the hospital where they take sick people. Dear God, make the people in the hospital feel better."

5. ***Going on a Walk.*** "Look at all the things God made — the birds, grass, bugs, and dogs. God made these things for you and me, to make us smile and be happy"; "Look at this funny leaf of clover! One is for the Father, one is for the Son, and this one is for the Holy Spirit. Amen!"; or "Let's see who can get to that tree first. It is nice that God gave us legs so that we can run fast."

6. ***Nighttime Examples.*** Many parents say the "sandman" came to visit at night and left "goo-goo" in their child's eyes. How scary! A man came into the room at night? No wonder a child is frightened at night! Try this instead: "Your guardian angel came to visit and check on you. Your guardian angel is one of God's most special friends who helps God take care of you. Your angel saw you sleeping and told God you were fine." Another idea is to let your child fall asleep to quiet music or stories on tape. There are excellent tapes with Catholic songs and stories available.

The possibilities and opportunities are countless! Looking for and thinking about God throughout your day will be rewarding and pleasing to your child — and to you and to God, too! Don't be surprised if you become emotional as your own relationship with God continues to grow through these continual, prayerful conversations. Be thankful!

Pray for Children

For Your Own Child

Pray for your own child constantly. Let him hear you praying to God. He will learn to know your love for him and for God.

- "Thank you, God, for lending me this precious soul. Help me make my child pleasing to you so that he can spend eternity with You in Your kingdom."
- "Let him love You, honor You, and worship You his entire life."
- "Help our family imitate the Holy Family in our day-to-day life, especially in our obedience and love for You."
- "Help me be more like Mary, Our Blessed Mother. Let me love and teach my child the way she loved and taught Jesus when He was young. She's my perfect example!"

Constantly offer prayers such as these for your child. Offer your day for him before your feet hit the floor in the morning. Ask for Mary's help. She will help you become efficient and motivated in your daily duties. Continually sacrifice and offer your daily duties — such as laundry, cleaning, and cooking — for your child. Pray while driving to the grocery store, playing games with your child, or changing a diaper. Pray anytime! Do this especially when you are tired. Your reward will be great!

Bless Your Child

Bless your child. Bless him often. Use holy water, if you have some. If you do not have it in your home, it should be available from your church. If not, take some water to your priest and ask him to bless it.

Bless your child when he is quiet or when you are rocking him, holding him, or kissing him good night. Make a small cross on his forehead with your thumb, and say, "May God the Father, the Son, and the Holy Spirit bless you, take care of you, and help you every day."

Pray for All Children

There are millions and millions of children who need prayers. There can never be too many prayers for children. Prayers never go unheard! We should be particularly mindful of:

- Children whose parents, siblings, or other role models are leading them astray by a poor example.
- Children who do not know God.
- Children who do not have parents.
- Children who are aborted.
- Children who are hungry, naked, or homeless.
- Children who are abused, physically or mentally.
- Children who are neglected.
- Children who are ill, especially the seriously ill.
- Children who are handicapped — and their families.
- All children, including yours.
- All families, that they may live in peace.

Praying for Your Child's Future

Pray for your child's future. God knows all. He knows the people who will be crossing your child's path tomorrow. Pray for your child's future teachers and playmates.

Pray that your child be receptive and excited about the places he will go. If he is to be a doctor or a nurse, let him be receptive and excited about science now. If he is to be an accountant or bookkeeper, let him excel in math now. If he is to be a spouse or parent, pray for him in this vocation also. Whether his duties be professional, spiritual, or otherwise, lay a good foundation early so that he will be good in his vocation later.

If it's God's will that your child be a priest, religious brother or sister, pray that your child hears His call and responds quickly and boldly, with humility and sincerity.

Pray for your child's future spouse. Pray that your child's spouse be kept holy and pure as he or she grows and matures. Pray that the parents are teaching about the Lord. Pray that the parents are setting a good example of a holy marriage.

Above all, pray that God's will for your child will be known to your child, and that you and your child will have the grace necessary to discern God's will in your lives.

chapter two

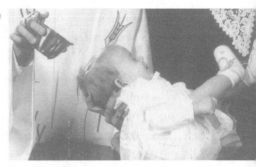

"Let the children come to me, do not hinder them; for to such belongs the kingdom of God." — MARK 10:14

'LET THE CHILDREN COME TO ME'

Baptism

With a Gospel command like this from the Divine, we must baptize our child and take him to Mass on a regular basis.

Besides being freed from original sin, baptism grants God's grace to a person. Grace is a wonderful gift from God that makes our soul holy. It also initiates the person into a lifelong membership in the Christian family.

In baptism, you (the parent) bless the child, profess your faith, and agree to raise your child Catholic. You promise to set a good Christian example, provide spiritual support, and offer religious education for your child.

Most baptisms are a formal ceremony, administered by a priest. However, anyone may baptize at any time if there is danger of death — and even in those cases when the person survives, a formal ceremony should still be celebrated in the local parish, presided over by a priest or deacon.

To formally baptize your child, you must attend an orientation session at the parish where you are registered. Then, schedule the ceremony with your parish office or priest.

You must also select godparents — usually two, one of each gender, though only one is required. The Church requires that godparents be baptized, practicing Catholics, 16 years of age or older, who have also received the Sacraments of Confirmation and the Eucharist. They are representatives of the Christian community.

They can teach and guide your child and provide support throughout your child's upbringing. It would be nice, although not required, if the godparent is aware of and participates in important milestones in the Catholic development of your child, including first Communion, first penance, and confirmation.

Baptism is a celebration of the beginning of new life. Celebrate!

You can invite family and friends to the baptism. Have a simple reception at the church or in your home. Include the priest with your other guests. You may also give small religious gifts to the child, such as a small crucifix, medallion, or a statue of Jesus.

Giving a small gift to a friend's child who is baptized is not only a nice gesture but also an outward sign of your support and love in the Christian community.

Baptism is special. It is a once-in-a-lifetime invitation into the Church, the Body of Christ, our community of faith. Make it special for your child. Take a lot of pictures, some for your baby book and some to frame for the wall. They will enjoy this as they get older, and may even "remember" being there!

Take Your Child to Mass

Taking your child to Mass does not mean taking him to the nursery or the cry room on a routine basis. It means taking him into the church, before the Blessed Sacrament, seated relatively close to the sanctuary, where he can see what is occurring.

Begin when he is born! Attend Mass as a family — with both parents and all kids. This may mean sacrifices, such as attending Mass twice because you have to be a eucharistic minister or sing in the choir. Family Mass attendance is essential. Sundays are holy days of obligation and warrant confession if missed without reason. And faithful attendance sets a good example.

Dress appropriately for Mass. Do not wear blue jeans or shorts simply because you've been dressed up all week. Instead, dress up for God, but do not dress down. You are on holy ground! Dress your child nicely, too. Make this a special day.

If the child is toilet-trained, make sure you take him to the bathroom before you leave home. Convince him that leaving Mass to go to the rest room is not an option. There are, of course, those times when this is impossible. However, you can usually tell when there is a real need, as opposed to his complaining "I've got to go!" after seeing another child leave Mass. You control the situation. Otherwise, bad habits will be formed.

When entering the church, allow the child to touch the holy water from the font and cross himself. This can be done from the first day of his life. When he is a newborn, you can cross and bless him with holy water. He will eventually ask why. You can then explain that it reminds him of his baptism while he is saying "Hello" to God.

Before entering the pew, have your child genuflect *with you*: "Let's kneel down together to say 'Hello' to Jesus, and let's tell Him we love Him." This may initially be a squat, possibly onto all fours. But it will eventually develop into a real genuflection. He will be participating, enjoying it, and making God happy. He may even want to go into the aisle several times during Mass just to genuflect. No harm done. As the child learns to talk, you can teach him to say, "My Lord and My God," as he genuflects out of love and reverence for God, who is present in the tabernacle.

While in church and talking about church and the Blessed Sacrament, use words like *reverence, adoration*, and *respect*. These are big words, but they are important — and your child will realize this from your attitude.

From the minute your child is born, let him participate in the Mass through your participation with him. Sing, respond to the readings, and pray into his ear. Let him *hear* Mass through you. He loves your being close and snuggling anyhow. Do not deny him prayer.

Explain to your child the meaning of the symbols, which make a Catholic church special. Start with the holy water. Point out the pictures and statues of Jesus, Mary, and Joseph. Look at the images in the stained glass windows. Identify the cross or crucifix. Comment on any pictures in the missal booklet. Point to the Stations of the Cross and briefly explain the steps of Jesus' Passion. See the banners used during the various seasons of the Church year. Look at the candles, choir, altar, tabernacle, and baptistery.

Teach your child to be observant and aware of the significance of the symbolism, colors, history, and meaning of all the items in the church. Someday, when your child visits a church of another faith, he may ask why you do not go there. You can refer to these many special items to help you answer his questions.

Perhaps he can wave hello and good-bye to Jesus on the cross, during the processional and recessional. Point out the activities taking place during the Mass. Let him hold songbooks and try to sing; this is fine, even if he can barely talk or hold the book alone. If he is small or does not become a distraction, he can stand on the pew while you hold his hand, perhaps dancing to the music. To God, this will be a prayer! Compliment him. He is participating and learning.

Make an effort to keep him from wriggling and being too noisy during the Liturgy of the Word. Explain that those people are "reading the Bible." Occasionally, the reader will mention names such as Moses, Daniel, or David, people he knows from reading the children's Bible. If you bring the children's Bible with you, you can quietly read parts of it. But do not get in a habit of reading to him during Mass. He can quietly thumb through the book and look at the pictures by himself.

If you go to daily Mass, he can participate by carrying the gifts to the altar. The "intentions" book is usually safe even if dropped, and he will be helping!

Allow him to put a few coins into the collection. Tell him that Father will give this money to poor people who do not have enough money to buy food or clothes. This is difficult for the child to understand, but less so than parish financing. It is a good time to learn that Jesus wants us to take care of others who need help. As the child gets older, teach him to set aside a portion of his allowance for the church collection. Teach him that God always keeps His promises, and that He has told us that our blessing for being generous will be returned to us tenfold.

Do your very best to keep him quiet during the consecration of the Eucharist: "This is the most special part of Mass. Be really still and watch Father. See, he is holding the cup of wine and the bread up to God in heaven so that God will bless them and make them extra special for us. God turns the bread and the wine into Jesus. Isn't that neat?" In a child's eye, this is exciting, as compared to simply reading and praying.

Holding him close to you on the kneeler and whispering in his ear during this time will usually keep him calm. This also will discourage his crawling on the pew behind you and bothering other people nearby. If he continues wriggling, say, "Shh. See, all these other people are being quiet. They are on their knees saying prayers. So let's be really quiet so we won't bother them, and maybe we can say some prayers, too."

Let him actively participate in the sign of peace. He can do this with you and all the people around you. If he asks you what this means, tell him, "You want all these people to be happy because they love God." As he grows older, explain that you are offering them "peace, God's peace, because you are forgiving them their sins. God is happy when He forgives us, as we confess our sins to Him. So He is also happy when we forgive each other."

Take your child with you to the front of church when you receive Holy Communion. Leave toys and books behind and fold his hands together in prayer. Take the pacifier out — but keep it in your pocket for emergency use! If you can hold him, you can even whisper prayers in his ear as you move toward the altar. He will want to receive Communion, too, and this can be difficult. But he will be cultivating a burning desire to receive Our Lord. If only more grown-ups had this yearning!

As the child gets older, when approaching the time he will begin receiving the Eucharist, he can begin to develop the habit of praying the Act of Contrition. When it is time for your child to receive his first Communion, a new prayer to learn should be a thanksgiving prayer after Communion. (See Appendix II for these prayers.)

The acronym *ACTS* can also help you teach your child what to pray after Communion. This may begin at age 3 or 4 in a simple way, so that it has formed into a habit well before first Communion:

A **(Adoration):** "Jesus, I adore You in the most Holy Sacrament of the altar"; "I love You with my whole heart and soul"; or "Father, I adore You and I lay my life before You! How I love You! Jesus, I adore You and I lay my life before You! How I love You! Holy Spirit, I adore You and I lay my life before You! How I love You!"

C **(Contrition):** Make an Act of Contrition. This can be a simple "I'm sorry if I made You sad, Jesus" or the memorized prayer (as your child gets older).

T **(Thanksgiving):** "Thank you, Lord, for. . . ."

S **(Supplication):** These are "asking" prayers: "God bless. . . ."; "Please help. . . ."; or "Please send us more priests. . . ."

A Few More Tips

Here are some other ideas that might be helpful:

1. Whisper prayers in his ear, similar to your nightly prayers, at appropriate times during the Mass. He can join with you if he likes.

2. Take religious toys to Mass, rather than secular toys. Have a "Mass bag" prepared in advance and kept in a special place where you can find it each time you attend Mass. Use it only for Mass, too, so it doesn't become "boring." Fill it with small statues of Jesus and Mary or a saint, a rosary, a small Bible or religious storybooks, and holy cards. Cars, dolls, and dinosaurs may sneak in, but hide them or replace them with others if possible. Do what you can to prevent the child's mind from wandering from what is important during this hour.

3. Bribery, or "positive motivation," works, too. Anyone who tells you otherwise probably does not have children! If you are having behavioral problems with your child, tell him there will be no donuts after church. Or perhaps say, "We can't go to Grandma's today unless you start acting nice while we are in church" or "If you are good, we can go out and eat hamburgers and fries after church."

    This is better than leaving for the cry room every time your child acts up. If you leave, he will soon learn he can manipulate you and avoid church by misbehaving. Remember, this is a last resort for poor behavior, not a routine punishment.

    There are times when a child cannot help the way he is acting. He truly bothers people around you. This is often predictable. His activities during the twenty-four hours before Mass may have caused it. Did he have a bad night? Did he miss his nap yesterday? Is he hungry? Did you rush out, missing breakfast? Is it 6:30 p.m. Mass on a holy day, so he missed dinner? Only you can be the judge of this. Some children are more active than others and need to go to the nursery for a month or two around 18 months. However, discipline and high expectations from you often work wonders. As long as *you* control when you take your child to the cry room, he does not manipulate you!

4. Attending Mass must be a pleasant experience. Remember, this is a child. You cannot expect adult behavior. However, be careful not to over-discipline, or else it will become a dreaded hour. Discipline with love. Use hugs; spankings will only make him angrier and cry louder. Compliment, praise, and reward his good behavior. Express your pride each Sunday, reaffirming his good be-

havior. It can be fun — and if he is bombarded with affection for being good, he may even want to come back next week and be good!

5. You pray, too! Make a special effort to pray during Mass. Not only will you set an example, but God will bless you. Never doubt, however, that you will be blessed just for getting to Mass. God accepts your sacrifice and understands the effort you made to get there. Just going is a prayer unto itself.

6. On Sundays when your child says, and really means, "I don't want to go to church today," your reply can be simple and unarguable: "Sweetheart, it's one of God's main rules He gave to Moses. We have to go to church on Sundays and say our prayers. Everyone in church is a family of people who all love God. This is the special day we pray together with this big family. Afterward, we can come home and play." Then continue getting ready for Mass and change the topic of conversation.

7. Begin your own family tradition that makes Sundays special. Sunday is the day we celebrate Jesus' rising from the dead. Only God can do that, and we want to praise God for it! Do something in addition to Mass, which can be a visible sign to your child that this day is special. For example, use china at your main meal. Light a candle and say a special prayer at mealtime. Gather *as a family* to read a few stories from the Bible during the day. Pray a family Rosary on Sunday. Be creative and think of something that you and your child will enjoy.

8. There may be a time when inappropriate behavior persists. The thought of the nursery sounds terrific. Take your protesting child to the nursery. On the walk, tell him, "If you can't be good in church and sit still and listen, then you

can't stay with me. You'll have to go with the baby-sitters." He will become angry. Next time he acts up, this will be an effective threat. Some children may want to go to the nursery. In this situation, the protesting child must be taken to the back of church or the cry room, instead of the nursery.

9. Ask for help from your guardian angel and from your child's guardian angel. Angels love to glorify God. They will offer help when asked: "Dear angel, please help guide my child to Our Lord. Help his behavior become that which gives praise to God."

Taking your child to Mass will become a joy, an absolute pleasure! It should be an integral part of your lives. You will watch your child develop and grow in his religion and his faith as he begins participating.

Church, Church Activities, and Almsgiving

Teach your child the name of your church. Teach him to recognize it from the street, always pointing it out as you drive past. Also, teach him to bow his head or make the Sign of the Cross as you drive past out of respect and reverence for Jesus present in the tabernacle.

Learn the prayer of Spiritual Communion (see Appendix II), to say each time you drive by a Catholic church.

Become involved in church activities, especially community-service work. Include your child in your efforts whenever possible. Find a niche that interests you, one you enjoy, of service to others. Then let your child tag along.

Become involved in children's education. If there is not a class for children younger than pre-K, you may want to start one. You could start a "play group" for mothers and their young tots.

Work on meal preparations for the poor and the sick in your parish, or for those with new babies. Attend pro-life rallies, nursing-home parties or visits. Deliver food or clothing donations. Visit and take some cookies to a grandparent or lonely neighbor.

Visit your church often, not just for Sunday Mass. There are dozens of reasons to stop by church for a minute. Drop off food for the poor. Sign up for helping with an upcoming event. Attend daily Mass. Make a "poor box" donation, letting your child make the donation.

Bring your child with you for all of these things. Explain that what you are doing is helping people. Helping people really makes God happy. Thank your child for being such a big help! As your child gets older, you can explain that these acts are corporal works of mercy. By physically doing these acts of kindness, we are expressing Jesus' love to those whom Jesus loves.

Be involved in all the church socials to which children are invited, including dances, ice cream socials, picnics, and guest-speaker functions. Let your child develop friendly relationships with other children and their parents from your parish. These relationships are healthy and fun. As your child grows older, encourage him to be involved as much as possible. He can be an altar server, attend Sunday school, and help you prepare for church activities such as Vacation Bible School.

Finally, the most important part: Stop by the empty church to visit the Blessed Sacrament. Do it alone with your child. Cross yourselves with holy water, genuflect toward the Blessed Sacrament, and then spend quality time with Our Lord. You can even sit on the floor near the altar. The child can say "Hello" and "Goodbye" to Jesus on the crucifix. Suggest that he say some prayers with you. You can sing "Jesus Loves Me" or "Away in a Manger." You can identify the familiar things around the altar.

Point out the things that make your church, the Catholic Church, special. You can do it more leisurely than you can at Mass, as described earlier. Do this often, explaining how special your church really is. Also, teach him to respect the sanctuary. The altar is holy ground. Running, jumping, and rolling around are not acceptable!

Find the statue of Our Lady and pray the Hail Mary.

Look for the special-intention candles. Light one and say a prayer. You can also follow the Stations of the Cross, which you have previously pointed out during Mass. These can briefly be explained, such as, "Look, Jesus fell down because He is tired. That nice man is helping Him" or "See how that nice lady wiped Jesus' face when He was hot?" This can be a great learning experience. As the child gets older, you can pray the Stations of the Cross. This takes only ten or fifteen minutes, and it should be done on Fridays, especially during Lent.

Be prayerful! Thank God for your beautiful child. Ask Him to open your child's heart to love Him more and more.

If an opportunity arises to be in a church of another denomination, point out what is missing. The explanation will help the child understand and appreciate all that the Catholic Church offers.

Taking Your Child to Funerals

Many parents fear taking young children to funerals. The common reason is that he is too young to understand death. First, who really understands death? Second, do the parents fear the questions the child will ask and feel insecure of the proper answer? Both are common concerns. However, death is part of life. It is an issue that must be faced.

The decision whether or not to take a young child to a funeral can be difficult. You know your child best, and you will have to decide when you can handle the funeral experience with him. A 2-year-old may be totally oblivious to the situation. A 3-year-old may be ready and able to handle the funeral. When does this maturity occur? Only you know the spiritual maturity of your child.

If possible, take your child first to a Catholic funeral Mass of a distant relative or friend. (Hopefully, you can do this before a close relative dies.) He most likely will not have been really well acquainted with the deceased. But there will be many relatives or acquaintances present that he will know. This is good.

Do not force it upon your child, but do not avoid the open casket. It is much easier to explain than a closed casket.

Explain that "this person got really sick and died." Have your child feel his own heart: "See? You are alive! But this person's heart has stopped, so he cannot wake up and move around anymore. It is really sad and we will miss him because we love him very much. That's why we don't play 'dead' with guns and swords, because it makes us sad. But do you know what? God is so happy and excited because this person has gone to be with Him in heaven. How does that happen? His soul went to be with Jesus. It's gone and his body is left here. Close your eyes and pretend that you see Jesus. Doesn't that make you happy? That person is really happy, too, because his eyes are closed and he is with Jesus."

If your child asks, "When can I see Jesus?" you could answer this way: "Well, hopefully not for a long time. God wants us to live, so you don't have to worry about dying. I would really miss you if you go right now. So maybe you can wait a while, okay?" As your child gets a little older, maybe 4 or 5 years old, you can explain what the soul is.

Relax and answer questions spontaneously. Watch your child's face for curious looks and draw out any questions. Do not leave him confused or afraid. Remember that your child still trusts you and believes whatever you say! Sound believable in your answers. Respond as best you can, remembering to do so simply and briefly. If you don't know the answer to a question, don't hesitate to ask someone.

Your child will probably do surprisingly well at the funeral Mass and the graveside service. Since you attend Mass regularly, there will be many similarities. Be open to questions anytime that evening, the next day, or weeks following the funeral. Answer them as best you can. There will be much learning and growth from the experience!

Remember, family members are around to help. Recognize that death is a part of life and can't be ignored. Finally, ask God to help you before you ever walk into the church. Ask Him to help you if you get a really tough question. Thank Him for allowing you this opportunity to teach your child more about Him. And when it's all over, thank Him again for not leaving your side throughout the funeral!

Taking Your Child to Reconciliation

Try to take your child with you when you make your confession. He need not go into the confessional with you. But if no one is present to help you, the priest will probably give you an extra blessing for bringing him along!

The message to teach your child is the importance of saying "I'm sorry." God already knows each of our sins and He loves us. But confessing them to a priest allows us to examine our conscience, express our sorrow, and receive God's grace and cleansing through the Church, which Jesus has appointed as the vehicle of God's graces.

Explain it this way: "We always want to make God happy. But sometimes we make mistakes. We sin. When we sin, we make God sad. So we go and tell the priest we're sorry, and God tells the priest to tell us that He loves us very much."

Use this opportunity to teach your child to say "I'm sorry" to kids or friends that he may have hurt. This is an important, often-overlooked courtesy. Your child will learn and grow from this sacrament!

Your Priest, Your Friend

Get acquainted with your parish priest. Become his friend. This is possible even in a very large parish.

Do what you need to do for your child to know the priest. This may mean going to daily Mass, socializing after Mass for a length of time, or spending time at the church during a weekday.

If necessary, ask the priest for an appointment. Invite him to your home for dinner. He may put you off because of a busy schedule, but if you continue to ask, he will respond.

This personal relationship is so important. Priests are descendants from the apostles and St. Peter, the Rock on whom Christ founded His Church. These are Our Lady's beloved. Never speak ill of them, and always keep them in your prayers! Visit them. Let them know you appreciate their work. Remember them on holidays and holy days.

Teach your child that priests are very special friends of God. They do God's work all the time. They help us and teach us to do God's work, too.

Then pray, "Dear Lord, if You want my child to serve You by a call to the religious life, so be it. Help him to hear and answer Your call. Always Lord, Your will be done. Amen."

chapter three

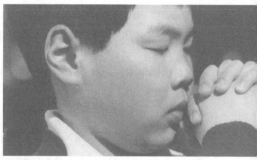

"These words which I command you this day shall be upon your heart; and you shall teach them diligently to your children."

— DEUTERONOMY 6:6-7

MEMORIZING BASIC PRAYERS AND SCRIPTURE

Introduction

The Catholic Church puts much emphasis on memory and knowledge of Sacred Scripture. This is evidenced by the extensive use of the Scriptures throughout the Holy Sacrifice of the Mass.

In addition to the first and second readings, the responsorial psalm, and the Gospel, almost every prayer — including the Sign of the Cross, "Lord, have mercy," and "Peace be with you" — is found in the Bible.

Do not let Protestants tell you that Catholics don't memorize Scripture!

Many of our Protestant friends do memorize a lot of Scripture passages as well, especially from St. Paul. Catholics can become intimidated because we can't always "pull up" a scriptural quote for our current situations. However, the passages are there.

A good Catholic scriptural concordance is a must for your home. It's never too late to learn. Begin with your child now!

Teaching and Learning the Language of Love

Communication is vital to any meaningful relationship. The more you talk to a friend and the more you get to know him or her, the more you want to know and share a friendship with that person. This is also true for our relationship with God — and this is just as true for preschoolers as it is for adults. What better way to introduce our children to God than to teach them to enter into dialogue with Him in Sacred Scripture?

There are many good reasons to expose our children to Sacred Scripture. One of the most important is to equip them to resist temptation. Do not deny that temptation exists for you and your child. It happened to Christ! After Jesus fasted in the desert for forty days and was weak and hungry, Satan approached Jesus and tempted Him with the treasures of the world (see Matthew 4:1-11). Three times Satan puts Jesus to the test, and each time, Jesus resists the temptation by quoting Sacred Scripture:

1. "Man shall not live by bread alone, but by every word that proceeds from the mouth of God" (Matthew 4:4) is quoted from Deuteronomy 8:3.
2. "You shall not tempt the Lord your God" (Matthew 4:7) is quoted from Deuteronomy 6:16.
3. "You shall worship the Lord your God and him only shall you serve" (Matthew 4:10) is a restatement of the First Commandment in Exodus 20:2-3 and Deuteronomy 5:6-7.

Clearly, learning Sacred Scripture was important to Jesus' mother, Mary, who must have instructed her Son as a child.

What a great example for us! Surely our children, when they too are weak, will be put to the test. It's not unrealistic for your kids to memorize Scripture verses for the majority of peer-pressure issues they will face in their young adult lives. Buy a good Bible concordance, and you'll find plenty of Scripture passages to address all the difficult issues your child will eventually encounter as a teen.

Another great reason to learn Sacred Scripture is to demonstrate our love for God. What would you think if a friend told you that she memorized — word-for-word — a love letter she had received? You would probably think she was madly in love with the person who sent it to her. We don't memorize Scripture to demonstrate anything to others, but we can do it as an expression of our love for God.

Finally, a knowledge of Sacred Scripture will prepare your child to defend and profess his faith. The Catholic field of "apologetics" includes the study of Sacred Scripture to support the teachings of the Catholic Church, especially those teachings that Protestants find controversial, such as salvation through faith *and* works, the real presence of Christ in the Eucharist, the Immaculate Conception of Mary, the Assumption of Mary, and papal authority. Memorizing Scripture to support these teachings will come later in your child's life, in his primary school and high school years.

It's not practical, realistic, or necessary to teach preschoolers complicated Scripture passages that deal with moral issues or apologetics. But it is possible to make knowledge of Sacred Scripture a regular part of your home life. You can start teaching your child Scripture at a very young age so that, when he enters his primary school years, learning the more complicated, more socially complex Scripture passages will be easier for him.

There are two basic ways to teach your child about the Bible: the first is reading the Bible, and the second is teaching him to memorize Scripture verses.

Reading the Bible

Reading the Bible to your kids is an absolute must for teaching them about God. It's His book.

Today there are many children's editions of the Bible, and most of them are fine for preschoolers. Younger kids will obviously respond better to color and pictures. Older preschoolers, however, will quickly lose interest in the overly simple versions. Try to stay ahead of their development so that they don't get tired of the Bible. You'll be surprised how quickly you can progress to the "real" Bible. Needless to say, there's a bit more material to choose from in the real thing than in the version for 3-year-olds.

One way to make the "real" Bible fun and less intimidating is to change the words or phrases to make it funny, more real, interesting, and easier for the preschool mind to understand. For example, when the apostles return to Jesus and find Him with the Samaritan woman at the well, try replacing "Has any one brought him [Jesus] food?" (John 4:33) with "Do you think someone brought him a hamburger with french fries?" Kids will get a kick out of it, have fun with it, and probably remember it better. The Gospels are full of lively, interesting stories that young minds can understand.

Memorizing Scripture

This is the difficult one, especially for Catholics. We have a tendency to be intimidated by Evangelical Protestants who have memorized Scripture verses. We may feel like we are missing a key piece of genetic material. But in fact, the only thing we are missing is discipline, the discipline to learn Sacred Scripture.

When you commit to teaching your kids to memorize Scripture, you will actually commit yourself to learning it. So just because "I didn't learn when I was a kid" is no excuse. Do it *together*. You've got to set the example. If you don't know it, you can't teach it.

Selecting Scripture Verses

The objective with young children is to keep the verse short and simple. If anything, pick passages that teach the love and mercy of God, or perhaps try working into your reading some scriptural support for childhood behavioral issues (for example, "Be kind to one another, tenderhearted, forgiving one another, as God in Christ forgave you" [Ephesians 4:32]). All you have to do is pick up a Bible and look for simple, loving verses. Here are just a few ideas of Gospel verses:

Matthew 6:9-13: The source of the Our Father.
Matthew 16:16: Who is Jesus?
Luke 1:37: The awesome power of God.
Luke 1:28, 42: The "source" of the Hail Mary.
Luke 2:14: The "source" of the Gloria at Mass.
Luke 18:16: God loves children.
John 3:16: Perhaps the most quoted verse by non-Catholics. Know it!

Ways to Memorize

There are many ways to actually memorize Scripture. In preparation, try writing down the passage in large letters and taping it on your child's bedroom wall. Preschoolers can't read yet, but they will before long. Scripture may even help them learn to read. Having posted it on the wall will help you with the memory work, too! Writing down and posting it will also give your child a wonderful sense of accomplishment, as he can actually see how many words he has learned.

To actually memorize the words, try one of these three primary techniques: repetition, rhythm, and rewards. Using flashcards, acting out verses, and linking together pictures (for example, using a picture of a bumblebee for the word *be*) are all helpful.

- ***Repetition:*** This is a very simple and common trick that allows you and your child to learn the verse one word at a time. After each word learned, you add an additional word. By the end of the passage or verse, you will have repeated the first words many times. Start with saying the first word of the verse, and then have your child repeat the word. Then say the first two words and have the child repeat both words. Repeat this until the entire verse has been learned. If you stick with it, and take just five minutes at a time, your child may learn the entire verse in two or three evenings. Here is an example using Luke 1:37:

Parent Leads	Child Repeats
For	For
For with	For with
For with God	For with God
For with God nothing	For with God nothing
For with God nothing will be impossible.	For with God nothing will be impossible.
Luke 1:37	Luke 1:37

Try using this verse for the next three evenings with your child. You will be amazed. It works.

- **Rhythm:** In addition to repetition, try making the passage fun for your child, spicing it up by snapping your fingers three or four times after adding each new word or adding phrases like "cha-cha" between words. Try giving the passage a musical beat or rhythm. You don't necessarily have to actually sing the verse; just give it a beat. Giving the passage rhythm makes it more fun and easier to remember.

- **Rewards:** A child will do just about anything for a Popsicle. Why not give him one every time he learns a Bible verse? As your child gets a little older, and the Scripture passages get more complicated and longer, you may find the need for a little extra incentive. Why not take him to his favorite water park, amusement park, or arcade when he (yourself included) reaches twenty-five memorized verses? Maybe a little sibling pressure would be good, too. The older child could help the younger child in order to get the "reward." The end in this case definitely justifies the means!

Summary

There are many great reasons for both you and your child to learn Sacred Scripture. It shows your love for God, prepares you and your child to respond to temptation, and it makes you and your child better evangelizers of our Catholic faith. But perhaps the best reason is that Our Lord tells us to!

chapter four

From childhood you have been acquainted with the sacred writings which are able to instruct you for salvation through faith in Christ Jesus. All scripture is inspired by God and profitable for teaching, for reproof, for correction, and for training in righteousness.

— 2 TIMOTHY 3:15-16

LEARNING TOOLS

Learning Through Hearing and Seeing

Books

Bibles: Most children love to have parents read to them. Before they are 6 months old, they are intrigued by colorful pictures. Your child also loves the quiet, uninterrupted reading time with you.

There is a wide variety of children's Bibles available. It is probably good to have two or three in your home, especially if you have two or three children! Have at least one Bible with realistic pictures; others can have animated pictures. These will be available at Catholic bookstores, general Christian bookstores, gift stores, and sometimes even in secular bookstores.

If at all possible, read the Bible at least once every day. Bedtime is always good because you have fewer distractions. Your child will go to sleep thinking about God! It's also good to read the Bible throughout the day, along with the many other books you read. It is okay if your child finds a favorite story and wants to read it over and over.

As questions arise, emphasize that the Bible is a collection of stories inspired by God, who is the real author. Within the Bible, there are stories about real people, not imaginary characters, who loved and lived for God. This makes the Bible different and more special than any other storybook. Because of the variety of stories and characters, this may become your child's favorite storybook!

Store the Bibles with your other children's books. You may want them a little to the side, but do not put them high on a shelf, restricting them for special times. Anytime your child picks up the Bible and flips through the pages, it becomes a special time. The more it is available and visible to him, the more he will read it. What a prayer in itself!

Exciting characters, good and bad, are in both the Old and New Testaments. Thrilling plots and colorful story lines can be found. Read about Moses both as a baby and as a man. Daniel in the Lion's Den, Adam and Eve, David and Goliath, Noah and the Ark, and other stories can be found in the Old Testament. The New Testament has numerous stories and events from the life of Jesus, beginning with the Christmas story and ending with works of the apostles. Jesus' parables such as the Prodigal Son, the Pharisee and the Tax Collector, and the Good Samaritan make great stories in and of themselves.

Children's Religious Books: Children love books and learn so much from them. Make religious books available to your child. Read to him often. Purchase children's books of short stories that have hard, laminated covers. Frequently, the pages are hard as well. These can be read to children younger than 1 year of age. Read books about the saints, and about saying prayers and things God has made. Find books containing simple, colorful, and lively religious poems.

Keep these books in a special area with the children's Bibles. Make sure your child can reach them and look through them anytime. Read the stories over and over. Make them come alive the same way you would Mother Goose! It will help your child enjoy them enough to want to search for them the next time he wants to read.

Often these books will be spread out all over the floor. Sometimes pages are torn. As long as they are well used, be happy. Thank God for His work in the mind and heart of your precious little one!

Adult Religious Books (Pretty Pictures): There are great religious books for adults that have large colored pictures. One adult book shows beautiful paintings of each of the mysteries of the Rosary. Colored pictures are in the middle of many adult Bibles and in books about the saints. Watch for them in bookstores. Keep these by your bed, or in another important, easily accessible place in your home.

Sometime, when your child is with you near the book, pick it up and look at the pictures. Tell him what is happening in a chronological, storybook fashion. Tell him about the saints and how special they are because they loved God so much. This spontaneous "reading" will be fun and different. You may find yourself "reading" the same books over and over. One day your child will begin to "read" it to you!

Audiovisuals

Both audiotapes and videotapes on religious themes are available. They may be more difficult to find, but it is worth the effort to find them.

If a Catholic bookstore does not carry these for children, or if their choices are limited, ask for catalogs. Also, check the general Christian bookstore in your area.

Audio: Religious audiotapes should become an automatic part of your drives in the car. The radio has very little worth listening to for yourself, let alone your child. Christian radio stations are better, but little ones may not be able to understand or relate to adult messages or music.

Instead, play some tapes with children's Bible songs. Find children's tapes with Old and New Testament stories. Your child will more than likely become fascinated with what happens next in the plot, just as he does with secular tapes. You may even have to wait until it's over at the end of a car ride before leaving the car!

Video: Religious videotapes are more plentiful than they used to be but still can be hard to find sometimes — but at least they are available. Many are only thirty to forty-five minutes in length, and they can be enjoyed in short intervals throughout your day. Both Old and New Testament stories are available. You can also find stories on Our Blessed Mother, on various saints, and on apparitions such as Fátima, Lourdes, and Guadalupe. As with any video, preview it before showing your child, checking for accuracy and appropriateness.

Having several of these videos available is terrific. Again, the child will become excited and entertained by the story. (See Appendix IV for a list.)

Singing

A child loves to sing. Singing makes him happy. It soothes him. Singing is also a form of prayer! Sing to him, and sing with him often. Add religious songs to his repertoire.

When rocking your child to sleep, add "Jesus Loves Me" after "Twinkle, Twinkle, Little Star." At Christmas time, sing "Away in a Manger" or "Silent Night." These may become favorites, and your child will ask you to sing them even into July! How beautiful!

Also, many audiotapes of children's Bible songs are available. Learn some of these and sing them at bedtime, too. Your child will enjoy the singing. God will enjoy hearing the prayers!

Growing and Learning

Reading and sharing picture books, singing, listening to audiotapes, or watching videos throughout the day will help your child grow and learn in the Spirit of God. God will become entrenched in his subconscious. He will be an important part of your child's life. How wonderful!

Your child will not fully understand all the nuances of the theological, symbolic, and other parallels and lessons of the Bible stories. However, as he hears them throughout the years, he will find more and more meaning in the story lines. Using the story of Noah and the Ark as an example, a child's interest and ability to understand may occur like this:

Age 2: He is interested in all the various animals.

Age 2 1/2: It rained, and the animals were safe in the boat.

Age 3: Noah obeyed God and built a big boat to help save all the animals. Obedience is very important to God!

Age 3 1/2: God put a rainbow in the sky. He was so happy that Noah, his family, and all the animals were safe.

Age 4: The dove brought back an olive branch, a sign of God's love. He gives us hope and promise for new life and new land.

Age 5 and older: The child sees the importance of being good, obeying God, and following His rules, the Ten Commandments. There are consequences to be suffered from not minding God's laws.

There are so many lessons to be learned! You will usually find more than one moral to each story in the Bible.

And there is an unexpected twist: Your child may come to enjoy these favorites so much that he will want to share them with his friends. You may find your child explaining to his buddy that Herod is the bad guy, and that the Three Kings are the good guys. You may be teaching other children and helping them grow in God, too!

Learning Through Touch

Toy Religious Articles

A child, especially a young one (ages 1 to 3), learns the most about the world around him by touching and chewing on toys. Why not, then, allow him this freedom with toys representing the faith in which you had him baptized?

Buy him six- to eight-inch statues of Jesus and Mary. Find or make a rosary that will not come apart at the chain links. At Christmas, find an inexpensive, nonbreakable manger with which to play.

If it makes you more comfortable, do not have the articles blessed. You will feel less guilty if something happens to one, such as going down an elevator shaft or out a car window.

Teach your child to respect these toys above all others. He can hold it, chew on it, or play with it, but not throw it across the room, jump on it, hit others with it, or use it for a weapon! For example, you might tell him: "This is Mary, Jesus' mommy. Take care of her so that we make God happy. This is a rosary for saying prayers to God. It's okay to hold it, but please don't swing it or hit with it. It's for talking to God, and it's special."

Store these toys in a special place. After all, they *are* special! They can sit on a shelf, on a kitchen cabinet, or by the child's bed in a special, predetermined spot. They could be kept on a small "altar" table in a special place in your home. Do not keep them out of reach. This defeats the purpose. And do not throw them in the toy box with the dolls and race cars.

Allowing a child to familiarize himself with tangible images is important at this young age. It will help him recognize Jesus and Mary in other places in your home, in church, or in books and Bibles. Repetition with a variety of stimuli to all of his senses will serve to reinforce what you are teaching.

Religious Figures and Statues

Have religious statues and pictures throughout your home. Place a crucifix in a prominent location. Place another one in your bedroom. Each child should have his own crucifix for his room. If two kids share one room, that room may contain two crucifixes! Make sure a priest blesses each crucifix. Let the child be a part of this blessing.

Also, have a nice statue of Our Lady in your home. Keep her in a special, visible place. There are also small, simple statues available of the Holy Family, Jesus, St. Joseph, the Way of the Cross, the Nativity, and many, many other holy images. You can continually add to your collection, sprinkling these throughout your home.

Religious pictures should be used as well. Included among the most precious are those of Our Lord's Sacred Heart and the Immaculate Heart of Mary. Beautiful prayers and blessings are also available, framed and ready for hanging in your home.

Begin when your child is an infant. Walk around and look at these pictures. If your baby is crying, show him the Sacred Heart, for example, and say a little prayer asking Jesus to help your baby relax and rest.

Your child will see these articles day after day. They are visible reinforcements of what the child is hearing from you. They add substance to an otherwise intangible subject. They make it easier to explain when they ask questions. Use them as a tool to help teach your child about Jesus, God, and Mary.

Altar in Your Home

Having a small altar in a prominent place in your home is a nice idea. This can be very simple, such as a small table covered with a cloth. You can purchase inexpensive cotton cloths in the Church-calendar colors of violet, green, white, and red. Here you can keep small statues of Our Lord, Our Lady, the Holy Family, or other saints, as well as a crucifix. Nonbreakable pictures, such as the Sacred Heart, could be displayed. You could keep your rosaries here, as this would be a good place to gather for family prayer.

Your altar should be at a lower level so that the child can see it.

Kissing Christ's Feet

Some children learn to give kisses before they can walk! This is how they first learn to say, "I love you." Nothing is more delightful for a parent than when this happens for the first time. Wouldn't it be delightful to Jesus also when He receives some kisses, too?

As you carry your young child past your crucifix, stop to kiss Christ's feet. Say, "I love You." You, too, must kiss Him, as an example. This will be fun because kids love to give kisses — and, as you can tell your child, "It makes Jesus so happy when you kiss Him!"

As your child begins to walk, you may find him running to the crucifix all puckered up! It's a good idea to place the child's personal crucifix in his room at his level. Hang it just to the side and below the light switch. He can "kiss Jesus" when he wakes up and leaves his room in the morning, as he plays throughout the day, and just before he turns out the light at night.

At times, you will have to use gentle discipline, explaining that "Jesus is so special and must stay hanging on the wall. You cannot take Him down and play with Him. He may break or get lost, and that would be so sad. So let's put Jesus back up, okay? Maybe we can find our little statue of Jesus to play with for a while."

Playmates who visit will probably become fascinated with the crucifix. They may never have seen one, and they will become curious. Use this as an opportunity to teach them, too. Take advantage of having the attention of one of God's most precious souls! Teach them, too, that "Jesus is special. He loves you so much. That is why His arms are open wide to give you a big hug. You can kiss Him if you want. See, we like to kiss Jesus. Isn't that neat? It really makes God happy!"

Giving kisses is a child's way of expressing his love!

Holy Water Font

Place a plastic holy water font near the doors you most often use, possibly your front and back doors. Hang it low so that it is within children's reach. Begin developing a habit of blessing yourself and your children each time you leave your home. Blessings and graces will follow you as God accompanies you on your journey, no matter how brief. A priest will bless a gallon of water for you upon request. This simplifies keeping your font full, while allowing you to be generous with your blessings.

Here are three helpful hints for holy water. First, transfer the blessed water into a glass container. The biodegradable plastic carton will eventually leak. Second, transfer some of *that* holy water into a used (clean), single-serving-sized water bottle with a pop-up lid. This will make it much easier to refill your fonts. Refills will have to be done often, because the water evaporates quickly. Third, identify your bottles. Take off old labels and use permanent markers to label your holy water to help avoid it being poured out or drank!

Stickers

Stickers are a favorite of almost every child. They love to stick them on paper, on their forehead, cheeks, and clothes. Sometimes we find them on windows and walls! Inexpensive religious stickers are available in Catholic and general Christian bookstores.

Allow your child to have a sheet or two on occasion. Use them to make pictures. He can stick them on pieces of construction paper. He can add to the artwork by coloring with crayons or markers. This is a simple craft that will occupy him, in prayer, while thinking about Jesus.

Put his artwork to good use. Use them for bookmarks for your Bible or other books. Hang them on the refrigerator at his level for him to admire. Hang them on the bulletin board in his room. Use them as birthday cards for family. Give one to a friend for a special occasion. Use your imagination with these pictures. Your child has laboriously produced them. Let them be his way of sharing and spreading the Good News!

Learning Through Play

Does your child play house and act out the parts of the mom, the dad, and the child? Does he pretend to mow grass or cook on a campout? If so, why not help your child play games that will help him learn about God?

Bible Stories

While out on a walk, find a stick.

"Hey, let's play Moses. You be the king, and I will be Moses. 'Let my people go from Egypt to the promised land.' "

" 'No.' "

" 'Then I will send frogs to hop in your hair and dinner. . . .' "

This can really be fun!

You can play Noah and the Ark with stuffed animals or with plastic animals in the bathtub, combined with tugboats and little people. Games and puzzles are available of Noah and the Ark.

Play and enact the stories that become your child's favorites as you read and reread the Bible.

Learning From the Saints

The ability to make, develop, nurture, and encourage a relationship with a friend is a special gift from God. With friends we share our sorrows and joys. We ask them for help and thank them when they support us.

The members of the Communion of Saints are special friends of God. They can become friends, confidants, helpers, and great inspirations for you as well as your child. You must learn about them. You must put forth the effort to develop a relationship with these friends.

The characteristic that all saints have in common is their love for God. There are many, many stories about the saints that describe the lives they led and their devotion to God. Many saints were martyred. Some stories are more animated, exciting, and suited for children than others. Your child will enjoy the story of their wholesome, devout lives.

You can find children's books and pamphlets about saints. Read a story to your child. Catholic bookstores can provide information on saints' feast days in the Church. Methodically read about the entire host of saints or select a few favorites and learn more about them.

Once you familiarize yourself with the saints, pray to them and ask for their intercession. For example, St. Jude is the patron saint of lost causes and impossible situations. Pray to him, "Please ask God to help in this situation." St. Anthony is the patron saint of misplaced or lost articles: "St. Anthony, please help me find the pacifier!" St. Maria Goretti is a model saint for boys and girls, helping them to remain pure: "St. Maria Goretti, please help me be good to my friends. Help teach them about God."

You can also teach your child about his baptismal saint. He can re-light his baptismal candle as you teach him about the person after whom he was named. There are many other ways you and your child can benefit from the saints.

As a friend, each saint is a gift from God. Saints are present in heaven for you and your child, as friends and examples. They do not diminish your prayer to the Holy Trinity or your devotion to Our Lady. They are helpful intercessors whom you are invited to know and love. Indeed, they are a reflection of God's love (see Appendix III).

Learning About Angels

Angels are pure spirits created by God. God made them to help Him. Some serve Him by acting as messengers and guardians over people. We know this is true, as angels are mentioned approximately three hundred times in the Bible. Even Jesus referred to angels in the Garden of Gethsemane when He told Peter, "Do you think that I cannot appeal to my Father, and he will at once send me more than twelve legions of angels?" (Matthew 26:53). We believe that each person has a guardian angel, who prays for him, protects him, and inspires him to do good.

Angels can seem scary: "Do they fly in my room and watch me at night?" Your terrified 3-year-old may never fall asleep! It is essential to depict angels as very beautiful, peaceful, friendly, and tangible. There is a picture called "The Guardian Angel" available through Catholic bookstores. This beautiful angel is watching carefully over a girl and a boy as they play. Place this picture in your child's room. Suggest that the child name his guardian angel.

You can teach your child to pray to his guardian angel. Ask favors: "Please ask God to help me fall asleep." In the morning and evening, you can say the Guardian Angel Prayer:

Angel of God, my guardian dear, to whom God's love commits me here: Ever this day [or night] be at my side, to light and guard, to rule and guide. Amen.

Finally, you and your child can spend time looking for angels in your children's Bible. You will find them in the Old Testament, in such stories as Daniel and the Lion's Den and the Fiery Furnace. You will find them in the New Testament at the Annunciation, when the angel Gabriel told Mary about Jesus. At Christmas, the host of angels appeared to the shepherds. And many Christmas cards portray beautiful angels with the Christ Child.

Angels are fun and exciting. Thank God for them!

chapter five

"And I tell you, you are Peter, and on this rock I will build my church, and the powers of death shall not prevail against it."

— MATTHEW 16:18

HOLY DAYS OF OBLIGATION

Each Sunday is a holy day of obligation commemorating the Resurrection of Jesus. There are other important holy days of obligation honoring important events in Church history. As Catholics, we are obligated to attend Mass on these days. Frequently, they do not fall on Sundays. However, this is a great and beautiful opportunity for you to teach your child. Here is a list of the holy days of obligation in chronological order by the Church calendar. (The obligation to attend Mass is abrogated in the United States whenever the Solemnity of Mary, the Assumption, or All Saints falls on a Saturday or Monday.)

The Immaculate Conception of the Blessed Virgin Mary (December 8)

Teach your child that Mary was conceived in the womb of her mother, Anne, without original sin. She was, and is, perfect. Mary herself confirmed this to the Church when she appeared to St. Bernadette in Lourdes, France, and stated, "I am the Immaculate Conception."

Christmas (December 25)

We celebrate the birthday of Jesus. More follows in the next chapter on ways of celebrating Advent, the preparation for Christmas, and Christmas itself.

Solemnity of the Blessed Virgin Mary, Mother of God (January 1)

This is a day to honor Mary as the Mother of God. Explain to your child that Mary is an advocate for us to God the Father. We pray with her and ask her help and guidance. She then asks God to hear and answer our prayers. Yes, God hears our prayers and can answer us directly. However, requesting Mary's assistance finds special favor with God, as she is very, very special to Him.

The Ascension of the Lord (forty days after Easter)

On this day, we celebrate the rising of Jesus into heaven in the presence of His apostles. This is often explained in the Easter books you read to your child. Also, every children's Bible has this story. Find it and read it to your child several times on this holy day.

The Assumption of the Blessed Virgin Mary (August 15)

Mary was taken to heaven, body and soul, and this doctrine is celebrated on this day. Although this will not be found in the children's Bible, it is pictured in Rosary books. The scriptural reference for this Church teaching is Revelations 12:1. This is the fourth Glorious Mystery of the Rosary. Tell your child that

Jesus loved His mom so much that He wanted her in heaven, body and soul, right next to Him — and it's true!

All Saints' Day (November 1)

A saint is a person who died and is in heaven with God. This is the day we remember the saints. These people have set good examples on how to lead a holy, Catholic life. Not all saints have been canonized by the Church. Was your mother or father a "saint"? Was a deceased friend a "saint"? Remember and pray for all people who have died.

chapter six

"Obey my voice, and I will be your God, and you shall be my people; and walk in all the way that I command you, that it may be well with you." — JEREMIAH 7:23

HOLY SEASONS

Advent

Just because retailers put Christmas displays up at Halloween doesn't mean that you need to do the same. Tell your child that it is not quite Christmas time: "After Thanksgiving, when we have the purple and pink candles in church, we can get our Christmas things out and start getting ready for Jesus' birthday." Continually talk about "Jesus' birthday," rather than Santa or other secular traditions.

The Importance of Mary

Explain to your child that the angel Gabriel appeared to Mary and said to her, "Hail, full of grace, the Lord is with you! . . . You have found favor with God. . . . You will . . . bear a son, and you shall call his name Jesus" (Luke 1:28, 30-31). Tell your child, "How special and exciting this must have been for Mary.

She was a *very* holy person. So God picked her especially to be Jesus' mommy."

As children get older, you can explain that, unlike other people, Mary was without original sin from the very beginning of her life. God prepared her to be the mother of Jesus, perfect in every way.

It is also important to point out that Mary obeyed: "She minded God." She said "Yes" to God's will. She could have said "No." Instead, her *fiat* resounds in heaven and earth throughout the ages: "Let it me [done] to me according to your word" (Luke 1:38). This is such an important lesson and prayer for each of us!

You can begin immediately talking about Christmas and its true meaning.

Advent Wreath/Chain/Calendar

The Advent wreath is a lovely symbol of the preparation time before Christmas. It brings your family together, encourages prayer, and escalates the anticipation for Jesus' birthday. It is a beautiful Catholic tradition that can be a great teaching tool for the entire family.

Each component of the wreath is symbolic. The circle means eternity and God's unending love. Tell your child that "the circle goes around forever. God will love you forever, too." The evergreen symbolizes everlasting life: "We can live with Him forever and ever!" The candles represent Jesus, the Light of the world: "The closer to His coming at Christmas, the brighter His light!"

As with any project, if your child can help arrange it, he will have more interest in its purpose and use.

Have your table set throughout Advent with a purple tablecloth and your Advent wreath. This will be one visual reminder throughout the season of your anticipation of the King.

Each time you sit down for a meal, light the appropriate number of candles and say a special prayer. This can be Grace Before Meals or weekly Advent prayers you will find in church or in Catholic bookstores.

The child won't want to wait until he finishes eating the meal to blow out the candles, but perhaps you can talk him into it! You may have to re-light them for each child to have a turn at blowing them out. This is okay, if it's fun and prayerful.

Watch the Advent wreath in your church very carefully. Each week a new candle is lit. You can compare this to your wreath at home. Tell your child each week that it's getting closer to Christmas. "When all four candles are lit, there are only a few more days left until Jesus' birthday."

Another easy Advent activity is to make a paper chain of purple and pink links for each day during Advent, placing a Christmas symbol, such as a manger, at the end. Put this in a special place, perhaps by his bed or on the Christmas tree. He can take off one link each day. His excitement will heighten as he anticipates Jesus' birthday! This also adds tangibility to an otherwise difficult-to-explain four-week calendar.

Advent calendars are also fun. These are available in the stores. But you can make them at home. One type of calendar uses two pieces of construction paper or poster board. The top sheet has doors cut out, which can be opened on each day of Advent. Behind the door is a small picture that is actually attached to the bottom sheet of paper in the area where it will be seen as the door is opened. Pictures could be simple Christmas and Christian symbols such as a candle, an angel, an Advent wreath, a star, a manger, or shepherds. Each day your child opens a door and talks about the picture. You can also say a simple prayer at this time, developing an Advent ritual. When all the doors have been opened, it is Christmas Eve!

The best Advent "calendar" would be a Nativity scene. The stable is already there at the beginning. Each day of Advent, add a character: lambs, shepherds, oxen, donkeys, and so on. On December 22, 23, and 24, add Joseph, Mary, and Baby Jesus. These can be purchased or homemade, or perhaps simply colored on a poster board.

Look for Purple (Violet)

While you are in church, especially looking at the Advent wreath, comment to your child about the use of purple. The candles and ribbons flowing from them will be purple. Father's vestments will be purple. Banners will be purple or decorated with purple ribbons.

Purple is a color the Church uses as a symbol of anticipation. Tell your child, "We're getting ready for Jesus' birthday! This is a time to get excited because something wonderful is about to happen. It's almost Jesus' birthday!" Purple is also a symbol of royalty, and Jesus is our King of the world.

Manger Scenes

The manger is the most important Christmas decoration and a true symbol of Christmas. Your child can learn a great deal from having frequent, "hands-on" access to a manger.

First, make him aware of the manger in your church. Go to the manger after Mass and look at it closely. Identify all the characters. You can retell the Christmas story. Begin by pointing out the angel of the Lord. Notice that Jesus is missing because He has not been born yet, and the Three Kings are missing because they come to visit Jesus after He is born. Then comment on the changes as the pieces are added.

Have *at least* one manger scene in your home that is non-breakable and kept within the child's reach. It can be made of cloth, wood, or plastic. The scenes come in a variety of shapes and sizes. Some may only have Mary, Joseph, and Jesus, while others have the entire collection of important characters.

Allow your child to touch and play with the characters. This does not mean that he is allowed to throw them or use them as hockey pucks! Help your child arrange the shepherds and sheep. Carefully arrange the cows and donkeys, making the appropriate animal noises with each. Make this fun! The Christmas story will come alive in his heart and mind. Tell the Christmas story, adding the figures as they enter the story. This could become a fun nightly activity while preparing for Christmas.

Some parents and educators suggest removing Baby Jesus throughout Advent and placing Him in the manger on Christmas Eve. This is a nice tradition, but it eliminates several weeks of "bonding" time for your child and the Infant. If given the opportunity, your child can become attached and relate to Baby Jesus — caring for Him, snuggling with Him, and kissing Him.

Christmas Storybooks

It is so easy to have several versions of the Christmas story available. Purchase some with realistic pictures and some that use cartoon style. Make sure the pictures are colorful and, preferably, the words simple.

Read these storybooks at least once a day. Depending on the book and the child's age, you can simplify the book by "reading" the pictures, not the printed words. If you read the story often enough, by the age of 2 the child may be able to "read" the pictures back to you!

Christmas Lights

When driving after dark, continually be aware of Christian symbols. Look for mangers, crosses, and stars of Bethlehem. Point them out to your child and be excited about his discovery of new ones. Explain that people put up Christmas lights because lights are pretty and bright, and that they are excited about Jesus' birthday, too! Tell him, "Jesus was like a light. He made people shine with happiness. So we put up lights because we are happy to be thinking about Him and getting ready to have His birthday party!"

Santa Claus

St. Nicholas was a real person — and a bishop! He was born in Turkey and died about the year 350. He is the patron saint of children, and his feast is celebrated on December 6.

This Catholic man was a role model of generosity and love, giving alms to the poor and teaching and loving children. He threw money through a window to provide a dowry (wedding money) for three girls. He had a special devotion to the Infant Jesus, once even risking his life to save His image from a burning church.

This is "Santa Claus." In the last century, advertisers, in an attempt to sell more of their products, took the bishop's miter off St. Nicholas and replaced it with a floppy cap. With humor and creativity — and looking at it from a commercial perspective — it worked. St. Nicholas became Santa Claus, and the rest is marketing history.

But it is your job, as a Catholic parent, to make sure that your child knows the story of *St. Nicholas*. It is also your job to downplay the commercialism and emphasize the historical reality of this holy man.

In many countries, St. Nicholas brings gifts to children on December 6. You, too, can begin a December 6 tradition in your home. Attend Mass that day, watch the children's video *Nicholas: The Boy Who Became Santa* (CCC of America), or find books with illustrations of St. Nicholas. Make the day special and different. Begin your shopping list for others by asking your child what he wants to give to family members. Try hard to eliminate the "I want" words from your child's vocabulary during this holy, giving season of Advent.

Start your own family traditions!

Nativity Videos

Allow your child to watch a Nativity video he would enjoy. Repetition is important. He will learn to better identify the characters as they are brought to life. He will also experience the greatest joy of all when Baby Jesus is born. This video can be kept with all others and viewed year-round.

Gift Giving

Place the emphasis on the giving of gifts, as opposed to the getting. Do not continually ask your child, "What do you want for Christmas?" Place the emphasis on "What special present should we get for Daddy or Grandpa for Christmas?" Your child can prepare a "give" list, as opposed to a "want" list. Then, let him shop with you. This may be slow, tiring, and cumbersome. But *giving* is the meaning of Christmas! God the Father gave His Son, Jesus, to the world. He was the Best Gift ever given!

A logical question you might hear is "If it's Jesus' birthday, why are we buying presents for all these people?" A good answer might be this: "Jesus is up in heaven living with God. We can't really give Him presents. But if we think about Jesus, then we can make or buy a present for Daddy. It really makes Jesus happy. We want Jesus to be happy. When we make others happy, He is happy. So we can buy a present or make a card for everyone who is special to us. When we see their happy faces as we give presents to them, we know that Jesus and God are happy."

You might be surprised on Christmas morning when you awaken and your 3-year-old says, "Oh good! It's Christmas! Now I can give Daddy his present and surprise him!" Oh, the delight of Our Lord when our young loving and giving children learn about the true meaning of Christmas from you!

Christmas

Christmas is the most exciting time of the year for most children. Parties, Santa, presents, candy, and more fill the season. It is also an exciting time for the Church — we celebrate the birth of Jesus! Teach this most important lesson to your child all through the season.

Christmas Morning — "Happy Birthday, Jesus!"

When your family awakens, remind your child, "It's a glorious morning! It's Jesus' birthday!"

Most birthday parties come with cake and candles *before* the presents. Why should Jesus' birthday party be different? Make a simple cake when you make your stuffing and pie. Let your child help decorate it with icing and sprinkles. You can even add a small plastic (or fireproof!) Nativity scene. Light a few candles, sing "Happy Birthday," blow out the candles, and *then* open gifts. Remember to take pictures!

Christmas Mass

Finally, and most importantly, take your child to Mass. This is essential as you celebrate what you've been talking about for four weeks! This is *Christ's Mass* (Christmas). It will be so exciting to visit the manger that now plays host to Baby Jesus. Churches often do a good job of including children in their Christmas liturgy. Allow your child to participate in whatever capacity he is invited.

In case your parish doesn't already have one, you could suggest to your pastor that a Christmas children's Mass be held on Christmas Eve. Have a script for the Gospel. Older children could be key manger characters, and the number of angel and shepherd participants could be unlimited. The younger children, ages 4 and under, could ring bells at specified times, such as when the angel says, "Glory to God in the highest" — and also during the Gloria. Your young child will delight in this participation.

Feast of the Holy Family

This feast of the Church is celebrated on the Sunday following Christmas. Point out a picture or statue of the Holy Family, read a story of Jesus' childhood, or read Sunday's Gospel at home. Turn to the Holy Family as the perfect role model. Ask for their blessings and for them to help guide your family to God.

The Twelve Days of Christmas

The Twelve Days of Christmas begin December 26 and end January 6, the feast of the Epiphany (in the United States, the Sunday after the solemnity of Mary, Mother of God, January 1; you could explain to your child that the celebration at church is just a little earlier — or later, as the case may be — but that it can be celebrated in the home on January 6). Try to do something special each of these days with your family to remember Christmas.

Have a prayer time each day when you "Thank God for letting Jesus come to us at Christmas." Light a candle, then blow it out following the prayer. Plan to stop by church and visit the manger scene briefly on each of these days. Say "Thank you, God, for Baby Jesus!"

Stash some inexpensive baby gifts in your house. Have a baby bib, socks, bottles, pacifiers, formula, and the like. If you have two kids, you could get twenty-four little gifts. Each day, after you say your prayer, have your child select a gift, wrap it (if you want to), and place it in a pretty basket or decorated box. On January 6, take the box to an appropriate recipient, such as a home for unwed mothers or Catholic Charities. You can explain the relationship between your gift giving and the Three Kings' gift giving to Baby Jesus. How happy Baby Jesus will be at this beautiful expression of love!

Epiphany

Although many people take down decorations earlier, the Christmas season does not actually end until the celebration of the feast of the Epiphany of the Lord, January 6 (in the United States, the liturgical celebration is on the Sunday after the solemnity of Mary, Mother of God, January 1). This feast celebrates the Magi's visit to the Holy Family with gifts of gold, frankincense, and myrrh. These gifts help explain gift giving for Jesus' birthday.

Some families have their gift exchange on January 6, as opposed to December 25. Another idea is to have a small family gift for each day of the Twelve Days of Christmas leading up to the Epiphany, a gift such as crayons or holy cards.

You may want to leave your decorations out until then. If not, leave out at least one nonbreakable Nativity set until the Epiphany. Let your child play with the Nativity set. Emphasize the three Wise Men visiting the Baby Jesus.

You may have devoted a lot of time to the Epiphany during Advent. If so, at least visit the manger in your church. Show your child what has happened. Explain that the church decorations will now be taken down.

Lent, Holy Week, and Easter

Lent, Holy Week, and Easter are by far the most important, special, and significant time of the liturgical year. Your entire family should treat them as such.

Decorations: Hold off on your Easter decorations until Holy Saturday, after Good Friday. Lent is a solemn time. You can "decorate" your home for Lent very simply. Remember the power of the visual! You can set your table with a purple tablecloth. A centerpiece could consist of a purple candle, a crucifix, and some nails. Change the appearance of your mantle. Adorn it with a purple cloth, a crucifix, and pictures of the Stations of the Cross or the Sorrowful Mysteries of the Rosary. Your child can paint, color, and decorate purple construction-paper crosses to hang in the windows or on the refrigerator. These are small, simple visual reminders for you, your children, and visitors of the season of fasting you are commemorating. Then, by the time you reach the end of Lent, Holy Saturday will be exciting (see the end of this chapter).

Easter Parties and Egg Hunts: Hold off on Easter parties and Easter egg hunts until Easter Sunday. It *can* be done! Save the joy and excitement for the Resurrection! (In some dioceses, the bishop may support an Easter egg hunt on Holy Saturday at the parish, or another location). You might miss the neighborhood or city hunt, which might give away the big toy or the most candy. Do not let the secular world tempt you away from your spiritual journey. This is a good opportunity to teach your children how special it is to be Catholic!

Lent

Lent is a special time set aside by the Church to help us focus on our journey to God. We should use this time to grow spiritually and "get back on track" with our faith.

Lent prepares us for Easter with the use of prayer, fasting, penance, and almsgiving. Holy Week begins with Palm Sunday and focuses on Holy Thursday (the Last Supper, including the washing of feet) and Good Friday (the entire Passion of Our Lord), including the Agony in the Garden, the Scourging at the Pillar, the Crowning With Thorns, the Carrying of the Cross, and the Crucifixion). Easter — the day Jesus rose from the dead — is, of course, the "grand finale," the climax of forty days of anticipation, the joy of our lives, the Resurrection!

Teach these things — all of them — to your child. This is the heart and soul of our Catholic faith! It is so important that the child learns this — all of it — at a young age.

Ash Wednesday

Ash Wednesday is the first day of Lent. It is a day of fast and abstinence.

- First, attend Mass on Ash Wednesday. This Mass will look and feel different. Violet will again adorn the altar, and often there is little or no music. During this Mass, the priest will bless the ashes of the palms from last year's Palm Sunday procession. He will then, with his thumb, place a black ash cross on everyone's forehead. He will say a prayer or a blessing such as, "Remember, you are dust, and to dust you will return" or "Turn away from sin and be faithful the Gospel." Your child will be fascinated with this beautiful tradition. His active participation will keep his attention. He gets ashes, too! What an opportunity to teach your child that this is a special time of year. Your ashes will also be a constant reminder throughout the day.

- Second, use this day to begin making unique Lenten "artwork" decorations for your home. Let your child color a picture of children or dolls, then put the black cross on their foreheads. This can be done to help prepare your child for Mass. You can also cut out violet construction paper crosses and decorate them with glitter, paint, paint pens, sequins, feathers, and ribbons, and then hang them in different rooms throughout your home. As your child gets older, you can even put a simple prayer or Act of Contrition on the cross and hang it on a bathroom mirror to recite each morning.

Ash Wednesday is a beautiful Catholic tradition that should be anticipated and celebrated with solemnity and reverence.

Lenten Suggestions

Make Lent special. This should be a time for spiritual growth for each family member, and the family as a whole. Doing religious and spiritual activities with your child and family is one of the deepest intimacies and can be a bonding family experience. But this will not happen without preparation, thought, and effort.

First, set attainable individual and family goals. What do you want to gain from Lent? Goals can be very simple, such as teaching your 1-year-old to recognize Jesus on the cross or pictures of Mary, or perhaps teaching your 3-year-old about almsgiving. Only you know the spiritual level and ability of your child. Do not underestimate him! He will anxiously anticipate Holy Week if you build his excitement for it. Also, do not ignore your own spiritual growth. Set goals to bring yourself closer to God. In this way, you can bring your family along, too.

There are three main components in preparing for Easter: *prayer, fasting,* and *almsgiving.*

Prayer is discussed in detail elsewhere in this book, especially in Chapter One. Do not neglect making prayer important during Lent. Set a goal to learn a new prayer, pray for certain special intentions, or pray a daily family Rosary. It is a vital ingredient for you and your child's Easter preparation.

Fasting is usually viewed as giving up food, such as chocolate or soda. But this does not have to be the case. You can "fast" from any earthly pleasure that is a sacrifice for you, such as no television or no telephone from six o'clock to eight in the evening. Offer this sacrifice cheerfully to God, and use this time for spiritual growth (prayer, reading, or family time). Self-denial is important. It helps us turn our focus to Christ crucified and what He sacrificed for each of us. It will set an example for your child and will help you, too. Your child can also fast, as you will see later in this chapter.

Almsgiving usually suggests giving money to the poor. It could also consist of giving used clothing or other items, or charitable works donated to someone in need. Again, setting an example for your child is important.

Stations of the Cross

Pray the Stations of the Cross with your family each Friday during Lent. This can be done at church alone or with the congregation. You can also make the stations at home using pictures or prayer books. In either situation, you should move from one spot to another for each station to commemorate Jesus' walk to Calvary.

Family Lenten Project and Calendar

Make a large Lenten calendar for a prominent place, such as your refrigerator. Doing so will remind you of your plan. This should be at least the size of poster board. Butcher paper works well, too. Since you are anticipating Easter, use purple markers and purple construction paper — point this out to your child, too! Title the calendar, "Lent: Pray — Fast — Give Alms."

Then plan something special for each of these components every day during Lent. Plan something for your child and something different for yourself. Put your intentions for the day on your calendar. Some suggestions might include the following:

Prayer: Select a daily prayer to say with your child. Find a special place to do this, such as on the floor near your calendar. This can be fun! Light a candle and say your prayer. This short prayer will be one he can learn and memorize during Lent. Learn a new prayer each year!

For yourself, select a different intention for each of the seven days of the week. Then, on each day, offer your sacrifice and prayers for this intention. For example: Sunday — End to Abortion; Monday — Peace in the World/Peace of Mind/Peace in the Family; Tuesday — Priests, That They Pray the Rosary and Remain Holy; Wednesday — Family (your child, immediate family, and grandparents); Thursday — Praise and Thanksgiving for Blessings; Friday — The Passion (contemplate the Stations of the Cross); Saturday — Home (blessings and peace in your home and all other homes). Another suggestion is to select a special intention and pray and fast fervently for this during Lent.

Fasting: Your child is too young to fast or to understand the purpose if you have him "give up" something. For example, abstaining from meat on Fridays may be something you do with him, and this is good. But he will not understand its purpose when he is 1 to 4 years old. Try this: Instead of "giving up" food for Lent, have him "give out" food. A lot of people do not have enough food, and this is more tangible for your child to understand. Help your child decorate a good-sized box. Use paints, construction paper, markers, or any fun medium. Then, purchase at least forty nonperishable food items at the grocery store. Include a variety of items. You may need forty items for each child, so think inexpensive! Then, prepare a special cabinet space near your other nonperishable foods to store these items. Following your daily morning prayer, let each child pick out some food — "only one" — and put it in the box for the poor. When Lent is over, you can then donate this box to a worthy cause. Your child can recognize the "fasting," or giving up food, from his own cabinet space as a sacrifice. What a great lesson!

As your child approaches age 5, you can add the true-sacrifice dimension and help him give up something tangible, such as candy: "Jesus gave up His life, and I can give up this piece of candy. I love you, Lord, please hear my prayers." They *can* do this with your positive encouragement. Set your expectations high, and they will be met! You can tell them, "Just think how wonderful the basketful of candy will be on Easter morning!"

Select a fasting sacrifice for yourself as well. Offer up every temptation as a prayer for your child or for your personal intentions.

Almsgiving: Almsgiving consists of giving generously of your time, talent, and treasure. This, too, is a very difficult concept for a young mind to understand:

- ***Time:*** Although this donation is for you or an older child, including the younger child is important. Time can be given by helping at church (office work, cleaning, gardening, etc.), visiting the elderly or the sick, or volunteering for your favorite charity. Offer your time doing these works of mercy as a gift to God. And take your child along. The elderly enjoy seeing children.
- ***Talent:*** Donating your talent can be fun and creative. If you are a good teacher, look for an opportunity to share

knowledge. If you are good at arts and crafts, teach a class of elderly people or make items to donate. If you are a good reader, spend time reading to your child's class. Find one of the special talents that God has given to you and share it with someone during Lent — and then offer it as a gift to God!

- *Treasure:* Playing with pennies is fun, and so is putting them in a piggy bank. So try combining the two. Almost every church has "Rice Bowls" — from Catholic Relief Services' Operation Rice Bowl — for Lent. These "piggy banks" for the poor are encouraged even for adults. Think of items in your home that you can count. Select something different every day of Lent and put this on your calendar. For example, after deciding to count all the doors in your house, take your child and count all the doors. For each item counted, give him a penny to put in the Rice Bowl. There can be four or forty-five pennies each day. It can add up, especially if you have more than one child! After Easter, bring the Rice Bowl to church and have your child give it to your priest. Explain that this money will be used to buy food and clothes for people who do not have enough money to buy their own.

More than forty examples of things to count in your home are: shoes in the closet, beds, windows, chairs, tables, pictures on walls, rooms, trees in the yard, lights, wheels on cars, ABCs, tiles on the kitchen floor, books on a shelf, audiotapes and videotapes, dishes in the dishwasher, silverware in the drawer, toys in the bathtub, stairs, steps to the mailbox, pages in the newspaper, clocks, pictures or statues of Jesus and Mary, ceiling fans, closets, plates in the cabinets, shirts in the drawers, games in the closet, keys on a key ring, eyes/ears/noses/mouths in the family, pens in the holder, fish in the fishbowl, trash cans, radios or televisions, play balls, coats or sweaters in the closet, kitchen cabinets, days in Lent, eggs in the refrigerator — and anything else you can think of!

As your child gets older, he can add part of his allowance to the collection.

Also, the giving of "treasure" does not have to be monetary. This is a good time to clean house! Not only are you preparing the way to Jesus' resurrection, but you can also donate toys and clothes to a worthwhile organization. You can also purchase new items to donate.

You should also select an almsgiving sacrifice for yourself. For example, take a donation to the poor box at church. The St. Vincent de Paul Society frequently has boxes, too. Even though your donation may be small, this can be a humble and holy experience!

Family Lenten Project Suggestions: Holy Week should look a little different on your calendar. Color a green palm branch or Jesus riding on a donkey on Palm Sunday. Maybe draw some feet on Holy Thursday. Then tell your child the story of Jesus washing His apostles' feet. Emphasize the importance of serving others. On Good Friday, highlight the space with red marker or crayon and tell your child, "This is the day we remember when Jesus died on the cross." You can also have a little picture of the crucifix in this square. You can find this on an inexpensive holy card. Put a picture of a huge white Easter lily on Easter Sunday, the day Jesus rose from the dead. You can even tape an artificial flower here.

Throughout Lent, your child will anticipate Holy Week. When Holy Week comes, he will know something is special and different!

Mark off each day on your calendar as you do your prayer/fasting/almsgiving project. Your child could glue a purple cross made of construction paper to the day you marked off. This is fun for him, and this definitely marks the day!

A reduced sample of a Lenten family calendar is shown on the following pages. This should be a fun daily practice. It will be a growing experience for your family. It may look quite different from year to year, as it reflects the spiritual journey of your family. It could even be an example and teaching tool for visitors to your home. Do not be shy or hesitant in explaining it to curious friends. You and your child will be touching others with Easter joy!

More Lenten Suggestions

Here are additional suggestions to make Lent a holy and happy time for your child — and for you:

- Read the Easter story to your child from a children's Bible frequently. Always begin with Palm Sunday. Read the entire story, ending with the Resurrection or the Ascension. You will be ending the story on a good, happy note, not simply "Jesus died on the cross."
- Help your child make a sign, a poster, or several small cards with the words *Gloria* and *Alleluia* (which are not used at Mass throughout Lent). Then hide the signs in your home. On Easter Sunday morning, bring them out for him to find, hidden amongst the eggs. This is a simple, fun, and meaningful tradition.
- Make a "good deed" or "sacrifice" cross. This can be made from sturdy poster board or purple construction paper and put on your refrigerator or kitchen cabinet. You can use stickers, or paint beans or pasta noodles purple for

LENT: PRAY — FAST — GIVE ALMS

CHILD'S SACRIFICES

PRAY — Each day pray the Children's Daily Prayer:

O Angel of God, be with me today. Be by my side forever to stay.

O Mary, I love you and pray, teach me to love God more today than yesterday.

O Jesus, I give You today, all that I think and do and say. Amen.

FAST — Take one food from the cabinet for the poor each day.

ALMS — Count the items on the calendar daily for the penny donation to the Rice Bowl. This daily exercise is an excellent way to take stock of all that we have to be thankful for, what excess we might be rid of, and what we are lacking in our home.

DAY	Sunday	Monday	Tuesday
DAILY INTENTIONS	For an end to abortion	For peace in the world, in oneself, and in one's family	For priests
ALMS — counting items for child	***Fourth Sunday of Lent*** Sunday Mass PICTURES ON BOOKSHELVES	SHIRTS IN DRAWER	GAMES IN CLOSET
ALMS — counting items for child	***Fifth Sunday of Lent*** Sunday Mass EYES, EARS, MOUTHS IN FAMILY	PENS IN DRAWER	FISH OR OTHER PETS IN HOUSE
ALMS — counting items for child	***Palm Sunday*** Sunday Mass SWEATERS AND COATS IN CLOSET	KITCHEN CABINETS AND DRAWERS	KIDS' AUDIOTAPES

SAMPLE LENTEN CALENDAR (final three weeks)

PARENTS' SACRIFICES

PRAY — Say a prayer for the daily intention on the calendar, make the Stations of the Cross with our child weekly on Friday at our parish.

FAST — Abstain from some earthly pleasure that we have chosen.

ALMS — Go through unused items in our house once a week and take them to the St. Vincent de Paul Society (SVDP), either at our parish or in our town.

 Use a purple cross to mark off each day!

Wednesday	Thursday	Friday	Saturday
For our family	In thanksgiving for God's many blessings	For an understanding of God's love — exemplified by Jesus' death for our sins	For our dead relatives
		Stations of the Cross, SVDP donation	Confession
LETTERS IN MAILBOX	FLOWERS IN FLOWERBED	CLOSETS	KEYS ON RING
		Stations of the Cross, SVDP donation	Confession
			PICTURES/ STATUES OF MARY IN HOUSE
TRASH CANS	NAPKINS IN DRAWER	PLAY BALLS	
	Holy Thursday Mass	*Good Friday* Good Friday Service	*Holy Saturday* Easter Vigil
TREES IN YARD			

Lent. Every time your child does a good deed or makes a sacrifice, no matter how small, let him glue or stick on his "reward." Try to cover your cross by Easter! You can expand this practice as your child gets older by offering the same prayers and sacrifices for a special intention. You could also decorate your cross with a Scripture passage that you would like your child to memorize. Each time he attaches a sticker or glues on a bean or noodle, recite the passage. Maybe you'll both memorize it by Easter!

Holy Week

Palm Sunday, the beginning of Holy Week, is celebrated on the Sunday before Easter. Explain that "This is the day Jesus rode into Jerusalem on a donkey. The people of the city waved palm branches. They spread the branches and some of their clothing on the ground for the donkey to walk on. This was a special carpet they made for Jesus because they knew He was special. They thought He would be their new king. But He was King of heaven, not just of their city."

Before Mass, everyone, including your child, will receive a palm branch to remind him of this parade. There will also be a procession in the church. Encourage him to participate. This begins to elevate his excitement for Holy Week. Your child may want to keep his palm branch. Keep it in a special place in his room, perhaps behind his crucifix, and it will be a visual reminder of this eventful celebration. Remember, it is blessed, so dispose of it properly (burn, bury, or return to the church).

You can also point out the absence of purple (symbolic of penance) and the presence of red (symbolic of Jesus' blood and His sacrifice). The priests' garments and the altar cloths will be red. We now remember Jesus' suffering and death.

Easter Triduum: Although these days are not holy days of obligation (except Easter, of course), they are among the most holy, important days of the Church year. We base our faith on what happens during Holy Week, especially during the Easter Triduum, which begins with the Mass of the Lord's Supper on Holy Thursday and ends on Easter Sunday evening.

Holy Thursday and Good Friday

Take your child to Holy Thursday Mass and Good Friday services. He has been preparing for and anticipating these days for a long time. You have been telling him about the washing of feet, the Last Supper, the Crucifixion, and kissing the feet of Our Lord on His cross for well over a month. Surely his curiosity and interest levels are up. These services will be the best possible illustration for young children to understand Easter. Our Lord does not want to scare children, and the services are not scary. They are sad and solemn. They set a mood.

You will need to briefly explain what is happening. For example, "Father is washing the feet of twelve people tonight (Holy Thursday) to remind us how Jesus washed the feet of His Twelve Apostles" or "Father is not consecrating the bread and wine today (Good Friday) because Jesus isn't here. We do not have to kneel down (genuflect) because that (the tabernacle) is empty. Jesus is gone today. He died on the cross. It's so sad. That's why the altar cloths are put away and there is no holy water in the fonts." Your child will surprise you. He will be quiet, attentive, sad.

Do not treat Good Friday like any ordinary Friday. It is the day Our Lord suffered and died for us. Your home should reflect this extraordinary event. Unplug your television and radio for the day. Don't answer the telephone. (Tell your family and friends ahead of time that you will be unavailable. If they leave an emergency message, you'll certainly return the call.) Also, say "no" to the neighborhood children at your door on Good Friday. Call the coach and tell him you can't make it to Little League on this day. Let it be a peaceful and prayerful day. Spend the day watching a movie on the life of Christ.

Make an effort for you *and* your child to venerate the cross at three in the afternoon on Good Friday, even if it is the one in your own home. It was the very hour of the death of Jesus. Try saying your Rosary, contemplating the Sorrowful Mysteries. Have your child color pictures from a coloring book of the Way of the Cross, and you, too, can meditate on the Stations of the Cross.

As your child gets older, take him out of school to commemorate this most holy, solemn day of the Church year. If both you and your spouse work, try earnestly to take a day off. This is valuable spiritual and family time. It is the consummation of the mission of Jesus, our God. Keep it holy!

Holy Saturday

Traditionally, this day, too, is quite solemn. Ideally, all decorations and egg hunts should wait until Easter Sunday. However, your preschooler has already been quite patient and done an exceptional job of celebrating Lent and Holy Week in self-denial and preparation. You have been contrary to the secular world, which has bombarded you from all directions with commercialism. Even many Catholic churches have moved their Easter egg hunts and celebrations from Easter Sunday to Holy Saturday. Do the best you can. At least try to avoid egg hunts before Holy Saturday afternoon. This won't be easy! This may be your day to pull out your Easter decorations or bake cookies — and, of course, to iron your Easter clothes to be ready for Mass.

Easter

Easter Vigil

The Easter Vigil on Saturday evening after dark is the most sacred of all Catholic liturgies. There is a lot that takes place during this beautiful celebration. Although it may not be practical to expect your child to be attentive or awake for the long evening, he may really enjoy certain parts such as the adult baptisms. The blessings of the fire and paschal candle are usually spectacular. You could plan on taking your child in comfortable "sleep" clothes with a drink and pacifier, knowing he will fall asleep. And you could always go to the cry room if he becomes distracting to others. Also, as your child gets older, he will know, recognize, and remember more and more details, opening the door for teaching moments.

What works for your family is up to you. But the service is incredible, memorable for all who attend, and definitely worth your effort.

Easter Sunday

When your child is very young, start Easter Day with a prayer.

Begin a family tradition! As soon as your child wakes on Easter morning, get down on your knees as a family. Thank Jesus for His suffering on the cross, but especially for being alive!

"Jesus is alive! Today is the day He rose from the dead. Isn't this a great day! We're so happy. Thank you, God! We can get all dressed up in our new church clothes for Mass today!"

Only after you pray should you look for eggs, eat candy, and go to Mass! Arrive early so that you can sit toward the front. Point out all the flowers and all the white. The red is gone! Easter is here and everyone is so happy! Look at the new clothes and the Easter hats. It is a time to celebrate!

Look for Easter symbols in your church. The Easter lily represents beauty, perfection, goodness, joy, and resurrection. It is shaped like a horn pointing to heaven, announcing the Good News! Light, such as the Easter (paschal) candle, is a symbol of Christ's triumph over darkness.

It's okay to talk about the Easter bunny and hiding Easter eggs, "the signs of new life." However, do not expect children to make much of a parallel between the secular and religious celebrations. As long as your emphasis is on teaching that the season is holy, you are doing well.

Have your child listen closely to the Gospel. It tells that Jesus is alive! Celebrate with Him and your family.

Easter Week

Easter is a fifty-day season, not just one day. Remind your child of its importance. Talk about Jesus being alive! Perform acts of kindness to "make Jesus happy." This could include returning your Rice Bowl to church or delivering your food collection to a worthy organization. You can gather around a new white candle, different from the one you used during Lent. Say a "Thank you, God, for Jesus being alive" prayer.

The Ascension of the Lord

As mentioned previously, this holy day of obligation celebrates the rising of Jesus into heaven. This is near the end of the Church's Easter celebration, which ends on Pentecost. Now might be a good time to put away Easter decorations.

chapter seven

You were running well; who hindered you from obeying the truth? This persuasion is not from him who called you. . . . I have confidence in the Lord that you will take no other view than mine; and he who is troubling you will bear his judgment, whoever he is.   — GALATIANS 5:7-8, 10

SECULAR HOLIDAYS

The word *holiday* comes from a combination of two words: *holy* and *day*. Thus, almost every secular holiday has a holy or religious history, purpose, or meaning. The secular world has changed the emphasis and celebration of some Church feasts. As observed in society at large, Halloween and, to a lesser extent, St. Patrick's Day are not the "holy days" of bygone years. The religious origin has virtually been eliminated.

However, it would do more harm than good to isolate your child from society by not allowing him to participate in these non-Christian ways of celebrating. If not properly guided, he will eventually learn society's ways and celebrate the holidays in some secular form.

Almost every secular holiday can be given a religious explanation. However, the Christian stories of St. Valentine and St. Patrick will not be nearly as entertaining to your child as all the valentines, candy, and the wearin' o' the green!

Find simple activities and provide simple explanations of the holiness of the day. Bring God into the secular celebration!

Also, remember your priest on the various holidays, especially Father's Day! Help your child make your priest a card, basket of candies, cookies, and the like. What a nice gesture! Your priest will appreciate being remembered, and he will remember you!

The following are a few suggested ways you can handle these days.

St. Valentine's Day (February 14)

Love is a special gift from God. On this day, we tell about our love and show our love to our family and friends. Give lots of hugs and kisses on Valentine's Day!

It would be good to tell your child that St. Valentine was a real person who taught people all around him how to love. Some people did not love God. They put Christians, like St. Valentine, in jail. But St. Valentine wrote letters to his friends about God's love, how to love, and the importance of love. These were the first "love" notes, and this practice led to the tradition of sending "valentines" to those we love.

Plan a special family activity this day. It would be nice to have a romantic dinner with your spouse. But it will be equally special to have a family "love" meal serving Roasted Love (roast beef), Crushed Love (mashed potatoes), United Love (peas and carrots), Red Rose (red Jell-O), Dreamy Love (rolls), Golden Love (butter), Deep Love (chocolate dessert), and Warm Love (hot tea or coffee). This may seem silly, but it will be great fun.

You can also read the parable about the Good Samaritan. Talk about loving your neighbor and how Jesus loves everyone, especially children!

Another idea is to make valentines with a "love" Scripture verse (there are many!): "Love one another as I have loved you" (John 15:12), "The greatest [virtue] is love" (1 Corinthians 13:13), and "God so loved the world that he gave his only Son, that whoever believes in him should not perish but have eternal life" (John 3:16).

St. Patrick's Day (March 17)

When your child gets older, you can discuss all the folklore and history involving St. Patrick and the conversion of Ireland. But when he is young, he will only see all the green and the shamrocks. It is easy to point out the three leaves of the clover, telling your child they represent God the Father, God the Son, and God the Holy Spirit.

Look for clover throughout your day, and continue to talk about the Holy Trinity. This is a prayer in itself! Decorate your home with shamrocks the week before St. Patrick's Day. Cut them out of green construction paper, and let your child paint, color, glitter, or mosaic them. This is fun, and you can talk about God all week in a new, refreshing way!

There is also a wonderful animated video on the life of this saint, *Patrick: Brave Shepherd of the Emerald Isle* (CCC of America). Viewing this on St. Patrick's Day will help keep the focus on God.

Mother's Day and Father's Day

When you attend Mass on these days, say extra-special prayers for the mothers, grandmothers, fathers, and grandfathers in your life and your child's life. Help him make homemade cards for these special people. If possible, spend those days with the mothers and fathers closest to you. Say "thank you" prayers all day with your child. Also say simple prayers such as "Dear God, please help all mommies and daddies love their children."

Remember your priest on Father's Day! He is the Father, the head of your Christian family.

Independence Day (July 4)

Thank God for His blessings on you and your family by letting you live in America. So many take advantage of this great gift! You can say prayers throughout the day with your child such as "Thank you, God, for America. Thank you for letting me go to church whenever I want." Sing "God Bless America." Have your child pray for the leaders of our country.

Halloween (October 31)

Many people have strong feelings about Halloween. With very good reason, a growing number of devout Catholics and conservative Christians are choosing not to celebrate the evening at all.

When most of today's adults were growing up, it was generally an innocent time. Most of our parents sent us out on our own to canvas the neighborhood for candy. Our trusting parents didn't think twice about letting us eat homemade goodies such as popcorn balls or candy apples. In our youth, the scariest decoration we might have seen was perhaps a paper-cutout witch.

Those days are long gone. Today parents must not only inspect what is brought home in candy bags, but we must also be on guard on what visual and audio images could be etched forever on our little ones' memories. Additionally, it is no longer safe to let young children be out of sight, even in the safest of neighborhoods.

The word *Halloween* actually comes from the term *All Hallows Even*, the eve of All Saints' Day (November 1). On All Saints' Day, Christians remember *all* the saints of the Church, whether canonized or not. The day after All Saints' Day is called All Souls' Day. This is the day in which we remember all the faithful departed and the poor souls in purgatory.

In centuries past, superstitious people were afraid of evil spirits that might be lurking around at this time. Thus came the tradition of carving scary pumpkins, hoping they would keep away the evil spirits. Other demonic traditions also crept in. Through the ages, Halloween has become the most "sacred" day for witches and devil worshipers. They gain more followers and offer more sacrifices on Halloween than on any other day of the year.

Deny Satan the recognition of "his day," and do not celebrate Halloween in a negative way! The following paragraphs will provide some fun ideas and help bring Halloween back to the literal meaning, the evening before All Saints' Day.

Costumes: Do not allow your child to dress as a little devil, ghoul, or anything remotely scary or evil. Turn his attention to God! Tell your child he may dress as a saint, Bible character, or other holy person.

There are so many exciting choices, including these: a shield-and-sword-carrying crusader for Christ; brave, young St. Joan of Arc; St. George the dragon slayer; Joseph in his coat of many colors; young David with a slingshot to beat that old giant Goliath; peace-loving St. Francis of Assisi; St. Elizabeth of Hungary, the modest princess who loved the poor; Mother Teresa with a love of the sick and poverty-stricken; Moses with that wonderful stick of his; Noah with an animal or two at his side; and beautiful angels, including Gabriel with his trumpet.

Turn this time into a learning experience. One mother mentioned that her child was named after Blessed Alan de la Roche, a great advocate of the Rosary. The child knew little about his namesake, so the mother used the month of October to research Blessed Alan. She went to their diocesan center and used the library there to read about this great priest of the Dominican Order. She then, in turn, "educated" her son on the man whom he was named after. The young boy excitedly dressed as the robed friar, complete with a fake bald spot on the top of his head. This was several years ago, and the young boy continues to take pride in his "special saint" and prays that one day Blessed Alan will be canonized by the Church.

Halloween Alternatives: Some parishes may celebrate Halloween with a "spook house" or other scary activities. If your parish's Halloween activities bother you, kindly tell your pastor your feelings. Encourage your friends to do the same. Perhaps, with a few adjustments and a little effort, a Halloween carnival could be turned into a fall festival.

If need be, create your own positive traditions. Plan a fun evening in your home on the same evening that others are trick-or-treating. Invite friends who share your beliefs. After all of your guests have arrived, in order that the party not be disturbed every few minutes, place a friendly note on the doorbell informing trick-or-treaters to go on to the next house. Your fall festival could include making caramel apples, bobbing for apples, pinning the leaves on the trees, and a candy hunt.

Incorporate All Saints' Day by encouraging guests to wear the saint costumes previously mentioned; have a fun "quiz show" to see how much the children know about the saints; say the alphabet aloud and have the children shout out a saint for each letter (X, Y, and Z are usually the toughies!); have holy cards and inexpensive saint medals for special gifts; color pictures from saint coloring books; have special snacks; and wind down by watching a favorite saint video. With a little effort on your part, this will become a very memorable and enjoyable evening for all!

Beware of "The Party Store": One of the most frightening places to take a young child in the month of October is the "party store," where both costumes and seasonal supplies are sold. In late September through October, children are exposed to various images of bloody body parts, animated latex rats, and ghoulish masks (perhaps with a rubber ax penetrating the head). Gory music is played, with moaning spirits, bloodcurdling screams, rattling chains, and creaking doors. As one 11-year-old says, "They try to freak out little kids." This is no place for your young children, who have a difficult time differentiating between reality and make-believe.

Older Children: Keep in mind that as your child gets older and more mature, there may be room for adult-supervised trick-or-treating. But costumes should remain positive. Always steer your child away from evil-related costumes no matter what the age.

Try to provide older children with additional "distractions" so that the whole emphasis of the evening is not on trick-or-treating. One elementary school teacher asks her students to make a candy graph out of their collected sweets. Students must count, categorize, and chart the number of chocolates, fruit chews, gum packs, and so on. This is a fun and educational activity for the big kids.

If older children want a few not-so-scary decorations, make it an educational experience. If they want a few paper bats or spiders, they must first research bats and spiders at the library. What is *echolocation*? How are spiderwebs made? These creatures are gifts from God and provide a great service in insect control. God's nature is not scary. It's awesome!

Whatever your activities are for your older children, be diligent in eliminating glory to the evil one. Be proud that your family chooses to glorify the Light of this world and not the dark!

Thanksgiving Day

Although the origins of this feast are from American history and not from the Bible, it can be a very holy day. God wants us to be thankful for our many blessings. You can spend the entire day being thankful for everything: from family and friends to all of nature — the animals, trees, and flowers. Your child can be thankful for toys, church, and even Jesus and Mary! When you say your prayers, take turns with your child naming things to be thankful for. How many can you think of? Most parishes have a Mass on Thanksgiving. Make an effort to attend, even if you are traveling.

chapter eight

But Peter and the apostles answered, "We must obey God rather than men."

— ACTS 5:29

CONTROLLING YOUR CHILD'S SENSORY INPUT

Your child's bright little mind is a blank slate continually bombarded with all types of stimulation. Some of it is good; some of it is bad. He is not able to discern between real and pretend. To him, it is all real. As a parent, you must continually monitor your child's sensory input, what he receives through his senses. You should constantly be aware of supposedly "good guy" cartoons, the evening news, the car radio, children's books and toys, conversations with his playmates, and inappropriate adult language and conversations.

Do you really approve of all your child's intake? If not, eliminate it, especially while your child is very young. At least do your best to do so. It will be impossible to eliminate everything because your child plays, goes to school, and spends time with other children who have been exposed to much more. You cannot raise your child in isolation, nor does God expect you to. But He does expect parents to be aware, and to control the message when they can. Christ tells us to be *in* the world but not *of* the world.

It is absurd to think that your child cannot grasp the reality of God in Three Persons because God is intangible. Think of Ronald McDonald. Your child has probably never seen the "real" Ronald in person, but he believes in his existence. He's on television. Ronald is imprinted on your child's lunch tray, his toys, and anywhere else where hamburgers can be promoted. If this can be reality to your child, then so can Jesus and the Trinity. With tangible stimulus, Jesus can be a reality for the very young.

Rule of Thumb: As you consider and pray about what you read in this chapter, consider the following thought: *Would you watch this program, play this game, listen to this music, read this book, etc., with Jesus or His mother by your side?*

Television

The average American has at least one television set in the home. And the average child watches television between four and six hours *each* day! This is sad but true.

As a parent, you must be very concerned about all the information your child absorbs from TV programs and commercials. He does not even have to be actually watching it for the information to penetrate.

Here are some thoughts and suggestions for TV viewing in your home:

- Remember, you control your television. You are in charge, and you set the rules. Whatever rules you make, your child must respect and follow them. Do not let your child talk you into more programming than you want him to get! Set your rules while your child is still young. One rule could be that he must ask your permission before turning on the television. Turning it on should not be an automatic reflex caused by walking into a room. Do not allow personal televisions in bedrooms. This leads to isolation from the family and hinders your control of what the child is watching.

- Be a good example. Minimize your own viewing time. You may be surprised at how much time *you* spend glued to the tube! Settle on specific programs you want to see, then turn the television off. Find an alternate activity. Remember that your actions and examples say more than your rules.

Television should not be a pacifier or free baby-sitter. Do not treat it as such. To do so is easy and convenient, yet it can be so harmful. For example, the cartoons are on television and it's time to make dinner. So you leave your child's side and escape to the kitchen. Meanwhile, the cartoons end and the news comes on. "Oh well," you reason, "it's just the news. What can be harmful about that?" Only murder, rape, theft, deadly car crashes, politics, and a host of other subjects not well-suited for a small child! Be alert. Either watch television with him or know what is on every minute. If his show ends, encourage him to play. Suggest that he help you with dinner. Minimize TV time!

- What about the commercials? They're awful! Commercials tend to lead a child to believe everything they see on television! Do you really want them to learn that a drug to increase the male sex drive can truly make them happy for the rest of their lives?

Not allowing the television to be a baby-sitter creates more work and takes more time and effort on your part. But remember that your child and his moral and value development will be worth the trouble.

- When your child does watch television, watch it with him on your lap and talk about what is happening as the story unfolds. Be ready to answer questions. Be ready to comment on poor language or poor decisions and actions by the characters. Express your negative reaction immediately: "That wasn't good for him to say that. It's not a nice word. Saying 'stupid' makes that person sad, and that doesn't make God happy" or "They shouldn't hit people like that (or jump off of the building, etc.). That's dangerous and can hurt you." If you are shocked by what you see or hear, or do not approve of the show, change the channel or hit the "Off" button! Your child may object, but simply explain what is wrong and why you do not like it. This does not have to be a lengthy or complicated explanation. Just say something like, "Let's find something funny instead of this sad show."

Cartoons

Are today's cartoons really okay? You probably grew up with the Road Runner, the Jetsons, Popeye, and Mickey Mouse. In the past thirty years, however, we have become more and more desensitized, as cartoons and most TV series have become more violent and spiritually damaging.

Recently, we've gone from Ninja Turtles and Power Rangers (who use weapons and physical strength) to Mario (who uses magic) to Pokémon. These "pocket monsters" allow children to have "power" or "control" over their friends when owning a certain card. This often becomes a *real* phenomenon, when children actually act out, or "play," Pokémon. But *who* has the power?

Mysticism, mind control, and Spiritism have become prominent. If you don't believe this, or believe it's an exaggeration, turn on the television and watch and decide for yourself!

As old-fashioned as it sounds, evil can creep into your home and into your child's little mind via the television. Evil is subtle. Do not diminish "The Power" of Jesus by exposing your child to a lot of the garbage shown on today's cartoons!

Much research has been done on the subject of television introducing and supporting negative influences on children. Many articles and books are available on this subject.

Thankfully, there are still good program choices. If you look around, you can find a variety of good shows for all ages. However, you cannot completely trust the programming of *any* channel. Be diligent and be careful!

Some popular TV choices for young children are "Franklin," "Blue's Clues" and "Little Bear," and old favorites like "Sesame Street," "Mister Rogers' Neighborhood," and "Barney and Friends," which are always faithful to both child and parent, with their simple yet fun lessons. They have given us years of enjoyment and education.

To minimize the amount of TV viewing while simultaneously avoiding confrontation with a child old enough to tell time, have predetermined viewing times. Generally, a child loves structure. It helps him feel in control of a world over which he does not have much control. Prepare a written schedule with times and activities (playtime, homework, feeding pets, setting the table for dinner, TV time, and so forth).

Saturday Morning Blues

Are Saturday mornings a battle between you and your child over which cartoons to watch? If you have a VCR, tape several episodes of your child's favorite show (of which you approve). Your child will not feel cheated. You will have peace of mind, and hopefully you will have avoided a confrontation every thirty minutes!

Does your child wake you early, especially on Saturday mornings, and want you to turn the cartoons on? Why not divert him from the inevitable? "Here, climb up in bed with me (us) and let me kiss your cheek a minute, let me get your piggies warm — or let's tickle Daddy." Suggest something fun. Then hug, kiss, tickle — play with your child. Suggest that you play board games or read books. This is a special Saturday morning treat not allowed during the week! This will be the best, undisturbed, quality time all weekend! Plus, you get to stay in bed an extra few minutes before turning on the television!

Start a Saturday morning tradition that requires getting out of the house — and leaving the television alone. How about going out for donuts every Saturday morning? Dad could take him fishing or to a fast-food place on Saturday mornings. Plan something fun that both child and parent look forward to. It can become a family tradition.

Family Activities — TV Alternatives

Family activities are a great alternative to watching television. It's no secret that we sometimes get into a rut with family activities. It is easy to just flip on the tube. There are many great family activities that are inexpensive, enhance family conversation, and please God.

Try walking, bike riding, baking cookies together, going to the park or zoo, going on a picnic, doing arts and crafts, participating in church activities, reading books together, planning a one-day trip, fishing, feeding the ducks, doing yard work or cleaning the house together, or flying a kite.

Go on nature walks and collect leaves, pinecones, and the like. Enjoy sports together — softball, baseball, soccer, miniature golf, Frisbee throwing, or tennis. Spend time reading at the library. Plant flowers or a vegetable garden. Visit museums.

Cyberspace Parenting

In this online, plugged-in, electronic age of information gathering and sharing, parents should be educated on the advantages and disadvantages of the phenomenon called the Internet. Through cyberspace, the Internet provides a vast array of information on virtually any topic humanly imaginable. This twenty-first-century information resource provides an endless database of knowledge. As with any form of mass media, it is the responsibility — "the golden rule" per se — of parents to supervise their child's access to, and use of, this encyclopedia to the world, just as you would television or video games. It is critically important that parents educate themselves and become very familiar with the computer and its capabilities in this new information age.

Here are some simple commonsense rules for parents to follow:

- First, turn on the computer. Yes, there are still many of us out there who have a fear of the computer.
- Second, don't be afraid to increase your knowledge. Go to your local junior college, computer store, or your local bookstore to inquire about simple "how-to" courses or "for dummies" books to get started. For the basics, you need to know how your computer works, basic word-processing and e-mail skills, and how to access programs and use the Internet. There are many companies and options out there to choose from. The companies have made it so simple that most of the time all you need to do is

pop a CD (compact disk) into your computer and follow the simple directions to get started.

- Third, once you know how to turn the thing on, call your local telephone company or check the daily mail for the endless Internet-provider solicitations offering free trial-periods and get plugged in. Many options are available, depending on your needs. The best way to gain knowledge about services is to ask questions of friends, colleagues, or even your local computer-store representative.

- Finally, place the computer in a central location accessible (in view) to the entire family, not in a far-off bedroom or office where you rarely venture. Although this may sound as if the computer is becoming the main focal point of the family, it will actually help eliminate unsupervised access and increase your own ability of controlling how the computer is being utilized. Also consider increasing your ability to control content and access by investing in inexpensive Internet-censoring software. The benefits will be well worth the investment.

There are advantages and disadvantages to the Internet. It all comes down to choice: choosing to supervise or censor the access and content your children are exposed to. The good news is that the Internet can be used as a wonderful resource and tool for increasing one's own knowledge of the faith; a tool for increasing quality family time; and engaging in an activity that your children are exposed to daily as they grow. The positive or negative results of Internet usage rest squarely on the shoulders of the parent. Lead by example. As a parent, you must gain the knowledge and engage yourself in the world your child is growing up in.

The positive side of the Internet is that many websites exist for virtually any topic of interest to Christians. What follows is just a sampling of some of the more exciting Catholic and Christian websites. These websites also contain links to other websites that provide an endless array of information.

Faith

www.newadvent.org (New Advent Catholic website)
www.ewtn.com (Eternal Word Television Network)
www.catholic.com (Catholic Answers website)
www.mirroroftruth.org (Catholic evangelization and apologetics)

Children

www.cccofamerica.com (CCC of America/Catholic entertainment)
www.bigidea.com ("Veggie Tales" series)

Sacramentals

www.rosary.com (website for the Rosary)
www.newadvent.org (New Advent Catholic website)

Movie Reviews

www.nccbuscc.org/movies (National Conference of Catholic Bishops)

The Bible

http://bible.crosswalk.com (Douay-Rheims version online)
www.newadvent.org (New Advent Catholic website)
www.nccbuscc.org/nab/bible/index.htm (National Conference of Catholic Bishops/New American Bible online)

Music

www.ewtn.com/rock/jukebox/jbrightframe.htm (Eternal Word Television Network/contemporary Christian artists)

Miscellaneous

www.mgardens.org (Mary's Gardens website)
www.catholicparenting.com (resources for Catholic parents)
www.osv.com (website of Our Sunday Visitor, publisher of *Catholic Parent*® magazine)

On the negative side of the Internet is the potential for addiction and exposure to offensive content. Both of these can be controlled and managed through simple adult supervision and monitoring. If you as a parent are engaged in your child's activities and aware of your child's habits and behaviors, this should not be an issue.

Another concern is the excessive use of chat rooms by older children. This is an increasing area of addiction for youths. Some young people now substitute the chat room for the normal telephone call. The difference is that a chat room is typically unrestricted both on access and content. This can also increase the isolation of older children from the rest of the family.

As society becomes more accustomed and adapted to the world of computers and the Internet, parents should engage themselves in the process and not let children pass them by. Today children are exposed at a very early age to the power and wealth of information the Internet and computers have to offer. Don't be left behind! Make the experience a positive one for the entire family. Show that you are genuinely interested in and knowledgeable about the Internet. Whether that is helping big sister gather information for her science report or researching a website concerning sacramentals, engage yourself and make it a good, healthy, and positive experience for the entire family. Don't be afraid to be called a "Cyber Catholic webhead!"

Books

What is your child looking at and reading about in his books? Do they have witches and terribly evil characters? Even stories such as Snow White, Hansel and Gretel, or Sleeping Beauty have their spells and witches.

There are thousands of books that do not involve mean characters, spells, and trances. Some good choices are informative books, with such titles as *All About Fire Trucks*, *All About Animals*, and *All About Colors*.

You must still review some of today's books. Some show the lead characters in Spiritism. Some levitate or stare into a floating crystal ball and project the future. Some go into a trance and give a crystal ball as a birthday present. At the age of 4 or 5 and younger, your child should not be exposed to magic, levitating, trances, or crystal balls, no matter how silly or insignificant it all seems! Also, why read books whose characters call each other liars, even if in not so many words? Why select books that talk about stealing, or that use words like *stupid*, *dumb*, or *kill*? If the book is good except for a few words, change the words as you read aloud to your child.

You must be aware of what your child reads, but *do* encourage reading! Give books as presents. Make going to the library a tradition and a treat. Most public libraries have fun areas with puzzles and learning toys set up for children.

Check into storytelling time at the library, where gifted librarians read — often accompanied by puppets or storyboards — to children. These story times usually are age-specific. There is a set time for 2- to 3-year-olds and another time for 4- to 5-year-olds. Each session has a topic such as bears, valentines, zoos, and the like. Story times are offered both during the day and in the evening. Maybe both Mom and Dad could go along!

As your child gets older, previewing and screening books becomes more difficult and time-consuming. However, it also becomes more critical as the subject matter becomes more advanced. There are some scary, adult story lines camouflaged with children's book covers!

Toys

Control what your child plays with while you can! If you are not sure about something specific, ask yourself if you think God would like this, or if Mary would let little Jesus play with this toy or read this book? You will probably get your answer quickly!

What about toy weapons? This issue is especially relevant for boys. No wonder our jails are full of men. We raise boys with toy guns, swords, army men, handcuffs, and the list goes on. Eliminate these toys as much as possible, especially when the child is really young. You can slowly introduce these toys as he realizes they exist. He will see them at friends' houses. Explain, in private, to your child why you do not really like these toys very much. Refer to specific situations that may have just occurred with the friend. Let your child know that these toys can be dangerous and hurt people.

Inevitably, your child will turn his finger into a gun or come home from a birthday party with a questionable toy or gun, and love it! Do not scold him. Talk with him about why you do not want him behaving like certain characters. Tell him not to point guns at people. Encourage conversation about the subject. If you do not discuss this with your child, he will participate and not tell you. Hiding his participation and lying to you can have terrible long-range effects.

As your child ages, you can introduce these characters and toys. Do it only when he can distinguish between appropriate and inappropriate behavior and when you can discipline him for misbehaving. Be consistent with your punishment when he does not follow your guidelines. You must punish pretended bad behavior because "someone will get hurt, and that would make God sad." Inevitably, someone *will* get hurt with one of these toys. Jump on this opportunity to teach your child!

You may have to allow your older child to play with these toys, or perhaps watch TV shows that have questionable characters, while your younger child is asleep. Tell the older child that his younger sibling cannot distinguish some of the issues until he, too, is a little older. Your older child will feel grown-up and important because of this privilege.

There are many, many toys that encourage positive behavior and aid in learning: Legos, wooden blocks, toy cars and trucks, balls, baby dolls, tea sets, puzzles, toy kitchens, and work benches with tools, just to name a few.

When friends and family ask what to give your child for Christmas and birthdays, do not hesitate to tell them the toys that you have approved and the toys that do not have your approval!

Movies

Be extra careful about taking your child to the Big Screen. Even with adult movies, the ratings can be misleading. Some "G" movies contain scenes that may be scary to 2- to 5-year-olds. Friendly monster adventures where the good guy wins can be really loud and intimidating in a theater. At least if you wait until these movies come out on video, the child has the safety and security of his own home, and distractions such as favorite toys around in case he gets scared. Think about it, and consider the delicate mind you are molding.

Also, many "children's" movies contain adult content and satanic undertones. Ask yourself: Would the movie be suitable for children if the animated characters were real actors?

There are good movies, but it can be difficult finding them. As suggested earlier, one option is to wait until the movie comes out in video. Rent it and preview it for the kids without their knowing it (so they won't nag!). You can also check the Catholic rating of the movie on the Internet. Then make your decision on its appropriateness for your godly children.

As your child gets older, you may allow him to see more movies. However, do not turn him loose! Preview the movie first or see it with him. If this is not possible, at least discuss the content with him.

When You Are Not at Home

When you leave the house with the baby-sitter in charge, you will leave basic information such as the number where you will be, the doctor's number, bedtime, and dinner and snack information. Do not assume that baby-sitters or relatives know your house rules. It is your responsibility to explain house rules. Here are some examples you may already have or want to think about:

- No TV viewing while the kids are awake. (You can't trust the commercials!) You can, of course, make exceptions, but you want to avoid letting the television become the baby-sitter.
- No boyfriends (or girlfriends) in your home.

- No movies on television or videos, especially PG-13 and R-rated ones. Exceptions could include videos you have previously seen and approved.
- No cartoons — and *only* TV programs you specify by name.
- No profanity.
- No long telephone conversations.

To a teenage or an adult baby-sitter, these may seem strict or "no big deal," but violations of these rules could prove damaging to a 2-, 3-, or 4-year-old. Just because you are not in the house does not mean that you have given up control of what your child hears and sees!

As your child gets older, you can learn a lot from him. Ask him what the baby-sitter did. If they were watching television, ask which shows were watched. This can be invaluable information. Make sure your child understands his first loyalty — Mom and Dad. If baby-sitters say, "Don't tell your parents," then they are undoubtedly hiding something. It is your love for your child and God's help that will guide you through this situation.

The Reaction of Friends

Be prepared for criticism from your friends while you "edit" what your child is exposed to. Your friends may say that you are being overprotective and unrealistic. So what? It is your beautiful, God-given vocation. Embrace this challenge with its crosses and blessings! This is your child, and the world will not protect him. So you must! You can modify your rules as your child matures and understands the issues at hand. This can be difficult, but it is so important for your child.

chapter nine

Be sober, be watchful. Your adversary the devil prowls around like a roaring lion, seeking some one to devour. Resist him, firm in your faith, knowing that the same experience of suffering is required of your brotherhood throughout the world.

— 1 PETER 5:8-9

REJECT TEMPTATION

Does your child have nightmares? Do *you* have nightmares? Are you tempted not to do certain things you know are good? Are there times you do not want to say nighttime prayers with your child because you are sleepy, or skip your morning prayer because it is a busy morning? Are there non-supportive people around you? Recognize these negative feelings and possibly difficult situations. They are temptations not to follow the will of God, not to pray, or not to teach your child your faith.

Teaching your child about Jesus and His mother will be very pleasing to God. Your relationship with the Holy Trinity and Our Lady will blossom and grow well beyond any of your expectations.

Remember, however, that anything pleasing to God will anger His opponent. Do not deny that the devil really does exist! He is mentioned throughout the Bible. Be prepared to be tested and tempted. Jesus was tempted, too, so do not be surprised if it happens to you!

Use Jesus as your example in handling the evil one. Like Jesus, when you feel temptation, when you sense the devil working on you, order him to leave: "Out of my home and my mind! In the name of our Lord Jesus Christ, get out of my heart and soul!" or "Get away from my spouse and my children. In the name of Jesus Christ, flee from our home!" If you use the name of Jesus, Satan is powerless.

If your child awakens from scary dreams, go to him and verbally bless him, crossing his forehead and praying to God to protect him. Hang a rosary close to him. Sprinkle holy water around your home while asking God to bless each room. It will keep evil away!

Finally, you can invoke the help of guardian angels — yours and your child's — who are always anxious to help "light and guard, to rule and guide." Also, recite the Prayer to St. Michael the Archangel, who is always helpful:

St. Michael, the Archangel, defend us in battle. Be our protection against the wickedness and snares of the devil. May God rebuke him, we humbly pray; and do thou, O prince of the heavenly host, by the power of God, thrust into hell Satan and the other evil spirits, who wander the world seeking the ruin of souls. Amen.

By your being alert, being prepared, and asking the Holy Trinity for help, God and His goodness will prevail! Do not — *do not* — be afraid! Be strong, be determined! And flee to God who will always protect you!

afterword

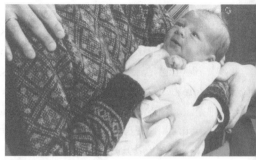

Husbands, love your wives, and do not be harsh with them. Children, obey your parents in everything, for this pleases the Lord. Fathers, do not provoke your children, lest they become discouraged.

— COLOSSIANS 3:19-21

WITNESSING THE LOVE OF CHRIST TO YOUR PRESCHOOLER

This book is full of wonderful parenting techniques to help your little ones come to know and love Jesus. "Doing," though, is only partly made up of the undertaking of special projects. It is, instead, primarily the time that fills in the gaps of life. It's living. It's going about our daily routine in such a way that is consistent with the Gospel of Jesus Christ.

For parents who are trying to raise children to love the Lord, it means "the environment" — the context and the tone that we set in our home. Perhaps there is nothing more important to creating this type of atmosphere in our home than the act of loving our spouse. There simply is no substitute for giving children the gift of living in a family environment that is happy and loving.

137

Let's face it. It's easy to love preschoolers: taking their first steps, making faces over new foods, learning to talk, "reading" for themselves (so they think), the first success in potty training, playing "catch," playing with dollies. You name it. They're a challenge, but they're also so much fun. And they love us unconditionally. Sure, we'll lose our patience every now and then, but overall it's easy to show love for creatures that love us so much and depend totally on us for their existence. Ultimately, then, just by loving our kids we haven't shown our kids much about loving as Jesus loved.

By loving our spouse, we can give our kids a much greater gift. If we consistently demonstrate our love for another human being that isn't as cute as a preschooler, and that doesn't depend totally on us for his or her existence, then we teach our kids to love when it sometimes isn't easy to love, and we've created a loving, nurturing environment in which kids can really learn. Without it, we've created a "do as I say, not as I do" environment. Kids can hear and learn all the right things, but if they're not witnessing it, it's not going to stick.

This, then, is our ideal for raising our preschoolers: Being Christ for our children by actively living out our Sacrament of Marriage, to love our spouse as Christ loves us and His Church. Our goal should be to never let our kids see us do otherwise. If they do witness us being unloving, our goal should be to teach the love of Christ through forgiveness, mercy, and reconciliation.

How, then, do we live the ideal? To be clear, this hasn't been a book about improving marriages. But regardless of where your marriage is at the present moment, there are some simple things you can do to create an atmosphere of true Christian love in your home. We've combined our thoughts into a few categories: *Communication, Affection, Play,* and *Prayer.*

Communication

Conversation is the heart of the matter. It's the primary way your kids see your marriage in action. It's present in everything you do as a family. You may be working around the house, playing, going to the zoo, having dinner, or traveling in the car on a family vacation, but whatever you're doing or wherever you are, you're in communication as a family, and much of your communication is verbal.

Here are some "tips" to help promote and develop loving Christian communication with your spouse:

- **Be respectful.** If we want our little ones to respect their siblings, playmates, and adults, we've got to respect our spouse in front of them. Focus on your spouse when he or she is talking. Really listen. Don't ignore.
- **Be loving.** This goes beyond being respectful. Being loving is hard work. Find ways to be supportive of your spouse in conversation in front of your kids. Pay compliments.
- **Be aware.** It's easy to say, and not easy to do, but we've got to be aware of what we're doing and saying — especially in front of our kids. Those little sponges won't miss a thing.
- **Be patient.** If you find yourself angry or frustrated, remember that the problem doesn't have to be solved right then and there. Wait until later to work it out. An ounce of patience will save your kids' hearts. Simply end the conversation with "I love you, honey. Let's talk about this later."

Affection

Kiss, hug, wink, chase, tickle — all this is the language of a preschooler, and we do it all the time with them. But do we do it at all with our spouse? It's all good stuff, and what a great image it presents to them of how Christ loves them! Your kids *love* it when you do it to them. They'll *remember* it when you do it to your spouse.

Showing affection to your spouse is wonderful, and so is "telling" affection. Husbands and wives can't tell each other enough — especially in front of their kids — how much they love each other, and the things they love about each other. There's another kind of "telling" that's also effective. Tell your kids how special their mom or dad is when Mom or Dad isn't present.

We have a friend who shared with us one of his fondest memories of his childhood. It was when his mom got out of their car at the grocery store while the rest of the family stayed in the car. While she was walking back with her groceries, his dad said, "Look how pretty your mom is!" He was 5 years old then, but the witness of his father's love for his mother has never been forgotten. Your child's experience will be the same.

Play

Hide-and-seek, wrestling, tickling, making faces, dancing — unstructured playtime, with both parents (with or without the kids for that matter), builds an environment of love, trust, and fun. It's great fun when Daddy gets goofy with the kids after dinner, or when giving them a bath. But throw Mommy into the mix, and you not only have more fun, but you also teach your little ones love, kindness, and joy — that is, the love of Christ.

Prayer

Another "must" is spending time with God and coming to know Him better with each other.

Praying for and with your children is the cornerstone of turning their hearts to God. All forms of prayer with your kids are wonderful. But it's so easy to skip group prayer with your spouse at night.

In family prayer, try praying for the other spouse, and encourage the kids to pray for both of you and for your union.

A simple way to pray for your spouse in front of the kids is to remember how Our Lord taught us to pray: *praise* ("hallowed be thy name"); *petition* ("give us this day"); *forgiveness* ("as we forgive those who trespass against us"); and *protection* ("lead us not into temptation"). Praise God for your spouse; petition God that you might be a better parent and spouse; ask God for forgiveness for the times you have not been a good parent or spouse; pray for God's protection, that you might be better in the upcoming day and to do this in front of your children and spouse. This is an excellent witness to teach each of you that only God is perfect and that even Mommy and Daddy need God.

It's a great idea to end prayer time with a blessing. Trace the Sign of the Cross on one another's forehead. Bless and consecrate each person to better prepare for God's work the next day.

Summary

The Church teaches us that the Sacrament of Marriage is an earthly symbol of Christ's love for the Church. A sacrament is a visible sign of an invisible reality. In marriage, this invisible reality is that Christ's love, mercy, forgiveness, and joy are real and available to each of us and to our children. Raising kids is not a sacrament. Your marriage is. Letting Christ live in and through your marriage, and submitting to His greatest hopes and desires for your marriage, will teach your preschoolers far more than you could ever hope to teach them on your own.

— DON AND SHELLIE GREINER

PRAYING THE ROSARY

Background

The Rosary is a powerful prayer to obtain the grace of God through the *intercession* of the Blessed Virgin Mary. It is a set of prayers divided into three groupings called "mysteries," which are events in our redemption. It is considered a prayer in honor of the Blessed Virgin and, in total (if prayed in its entirety at one time), consists of one hundred fifty-three Hail Marys, sixteen Our Fathers, sixteen Glory Be prayers, one Apostles' Creed, and one Hail Holy Queen.

The groupings are divided so that we meditate on the early life, Passion, and glory of Christ, and these events are called, in turn, the Joyful, Sorrowful, and Glorious Mysteries. During the Blessed Mother's apparitions at Fátima, Portugal, she requested that each decade be followed by a prayer, which has come to be known as the Fátima Prayer.

Ordinarily, one-third of the Rosary is said at one time. As we say each mystery, we meditate on our faith. The Rosary combines vocal and mental prayer. As you pray each mystery, you can also meditate on the "fruit," or the Christian virtue, related to that particular mystery. The Rosary is a summary of the most important parts of the Gospels.

The Rosary began in the Middle Ages, when many people could not read the one hundred fifty Psalms of David, which were (and remain) the basis of the Divine Office prayed by clerics and religious communities. To imitate this form of prayer, strands of one hundred fifty stones or seeds were made, and the people substituted one Our Father (eventually, one Hail Mary) for each psalm. The word *Rosary* means a garland, or wreath, of roses — an offering to God, in honor of Our Lady. The Rosary was later divided into the fifteen mysteries and decades we see today.

St. Dominic encouraged its widespread use as a tool to combat heresies. This led the Dominicans and other religious orders to adopt it as part of their religious habits. It was worn at the left side of the belt, where a knight's sword would be worn, as it was their "spiritual sword" in the battle against evil. Many graces and innumerable conversions have been won by its recitation. In recognition of the efficacy of this form of prayer, Pope St. Pius V instituted the feast of Our Lady of the Rosary (October 7) after the victory at Lepanto, in 1571, over Muslim forces that were threatening Europe. In several Church-approved apparitions, the Blessed Virgin Mary spoke of it as the most powerful weapon for good, asked for it to be recited devoutly and frequently by everyone, and promised that it would obtain many graces.

The Rosary, a Marian prayer, is a very Christ-centered prayer. Of the fifteen mysteries, only the first two and the last two even mention Mary as the central figure. But these four point out Mary's role in God's plan of redemption. Marian devotion is a necessary part of a full Christian prayer life. Such true devotion can always be known by the simple fact that it leads one to a greater understanding of, and love for, the Beloved Son, Jesus Christ. In this respect, the Rosary is the perfect Marian prayer.

What follows is a brief summary of the Rosary. There are many booklets with more detailed information to help you pray the Rosary. There are also audiotapes and videotapes available so that you can pray along with the narrator.

How to Pray the Rosary

Opening Prayers

- Make the Sign of the Cross.

Then pray the following:

- The Apostles' Creed (while holding the crucifix)
- The Our Father (on the large bead)
- Three Hail Marys (on the three small beads). These can be said for the virtues of faith, hope, and charity, or for the intentions of the Holy Father.
- The Glory Be

Prayers for Each Mystery and Its Decade

1. Announce each mystery on the large bead and say one Our Father. Then meditate on the announced mystery and its fruit (specified below in the listing of the mysteries) while praying the decade.
2. Say ten Hail Marys, one on each of the smaller beads.
3. Say the Glory Be (between the last Hail Mary bead and the next Our Father bead).
4. Say the Fátima Prayer (in the same space as the Glory Be).
5. Repeat Steps 1 through 4, for the remaining four decades.

Concluding Prayers

- After completing the fifth decade, say the Hail Holy Queen.
- Say "Let us pray," and then say the Prayer After the Rosary.
- Make the Sign of the Cross.
- Kiss the crucifix.

Some people like to begin the Rosary with the Memorare of St. Bernard and end with the Prayer to St. Michael the Archangel. These beautiful prayer options can be found in Appendix II.

Rosary Prayers

Apostles' Creed

I believe in God, the Father almighty, creator of heaven and earth; and in Jesus Christ, his only Son, our Lord; who was conceived by the Holy Spirit, born of the Virgin Mary, suffered under Pontius Pilate, was crucified, died, and was buried. He descended into hell; the third day he arose again from the dead; he ascended into heaven and sits at the right hand of God the Father almighty; from thence he shall come to judge the living and the dead. I believe in the Holy Spirit, the holy Catholic Church, the communion of saints, the forgiveness of sins, the resurrection of the body, and life everlasting. Amen.

Our Father

Our Father, who art in heaven, hallowed be thy name; thy kingdom come; thy will be done on earth as it is in heaven. Give us this day our daily bread; and forgive us our trespasses as we forgive those who trespass against us; and lead us not into temptation, but deliver us from evil. Amen.

Hail Mary

Hail Mary, full of grace; the Lord is with thee. Blessed art thou among women, and blessed is the fruit of thy womb, Jesus. Holy Mary, Mother of God, pray for us sinners, now and at the hour of our death. Amen.

Glory Be

Glory be to the Father, and to the Son, and to the Holy Spirit. As it was in the beginning, is now, and ever shall be, world without end. Amen.

Fátima Prayer

O my Jesus, forgive us our sins; save us from the fires of hell. Lead all souls to heaven, especially those in most need of thy mercy.

Hail Holy Queen

Hail, holy Queen, mother of mercy: our life, our sweetness, and our hope. To thee do we cry, poor, banished children of Eve. To thee do we send up our sighs, mourning, and weeping in this valley of tears. Turn then, most gracious advocate, thine eyes of mercy toward us, and after this our exile show unto us the blessed fruit of thy womb, Jesus. O clement, O loving, O sweet Virgin Mary.

V. Pray for us, O holy Mother of God.

R. That we may be made worthy of the promises of Christ.

Prayer After the Rosary

O God, whose only begotten Son, by his life, death and resurrection, has purchased for us the rewards of eternal life; grant we beseech thee, that by meditating upon these mysteries of the Most Holy Rosary of the Blessed Virgin Mary, that we may imitate what they contain and obtain what they promise, through the same Christ our Lord. Amen.

The Mysteries of the Rosary

The Joyful Mysteries

To be prayed on Mondays and Thursdays and all Sundays of Advent.

1. *The Annunciation.* Mary learns from the angel Gabriel that God wishes her to become the Mother of God, and she humbly accepts (see Luke 1:26-38). Fruit of the mystery: *humility.*
2. *The Visitation.* Mary goes to visit her cousin Elizabeth and is hailed as "blessed" (see Luke 1:39-56). Fruit of the mystery: *fraternal charity.*
3. *The Nativity.* Mary gives birth to Jesus in a stable at Bethlehem (see Luke 2:1-20). Fruit of the mystery: *esteem for spiritual values.*
4. *The Presentation.* Mary and Joseph present Jesus to His heavenly Father in the Temple according to Jewish law (see Luke 2:22-39). Fruits of the mystery: *purity and obedience.*
5. *The Finding in the Temple.* After searching for three days, Mary and Joseph find Jesus teaching in the Temple (see Luke 2:41-52). Fruit of the mystery: *fidelity to one's duties.*

The Sorrowful Mysteries

To be prayed on Tuesdays and Fridays and all Sundays of Lent.

1. ***The Agony in the Garden.*** Thoughts of our sins and His coming sufferings cause our Savior to sweat blood (see Luke 22:39-46; also Matthew 26:36-46 and Mark 14:32-42). Fruit of the mystery: *sorrow for our sins.*

2. ***The Scourging at the Pillar.*** Jesus is stripped and unmercifully scourged until His body is one mass of bloody wounds (see Matthew 27:26; also Mark 15:15 and John 19:1). Fruit of the mystery: *mortification of the senses.*

3. ***The Crowning with Thorns.*** Jesus' claim to Kingship is ridiculed by soldiers who place a crown of thorns on His head and a reed in His hand (see Matthew 27:27-31; also Mark 15:16-20 and John 19:2-3). Fruit of the mystery: *love for humiliations.*

4. ***The Carrying of the Cross.*** Jesus accepts His cross and makes His way to the place of crucifixion, while Mary follows Him sorrowfully (see Luke 23: 26-32; also Matthew 27:32, Mark 15:21, and John 19:16-17). Fruit of the mystery: *bearing of trials.*

5. ***The Crucifixion.*** Jesus dies, nailed to the cross, after hours of agony witnessed by His mother (see John 19:18-30; also Matthew 27: 33-50, Mark 15:24-37, and Luke 23:33-46). Fruit of the mystery: *forgiveness of injuries.*

The Glorious Mysteries

To be prayed on Wednesdays and Saturdays and all Sundays (except the Sundays of Advent and Lent).

1. ***The Resurrection.*** Jesus rises from the dead on Easter Sunday, glorious and immortal (see Matthew 28:1-10; also Mark 16:2-9, Luke 24:1-12, and John 20:1-17). Fruits of the mystery: *faith and hope.*

2. ***The Ascension.*** Jesus ascends into heaven forty days after His resurrection to sit at the right hand of God the Father, from whence He shall return to judge the living and the dead (see Luke 24: 50-51; also Mark 16:19 and Acts 1:1-9). Fruit of the mystery: *desire for heaven.*

3. ***The Descent of the Holy Spirit.*** Jesus sends the Holy Spirit in the form of fiery tongues upon His apostles and disciples (see Acts: 2:1-4). Fruits of the mystery: *the Seven Gifts of the Holy Spirit (understanding, wisdom, counsel, knowledge, fortitude, piety, and fear of the Lord).*

4. ***The Assumption.*** Mary is taken up body and soul to God (see Revelation 12:1). Fruit of the mystery: *devotion to Mary.*

5. ***The Coronation.*** Mary is crowned as Queen of Heaven and Earth, that she may rule over all hearts in time and eternity (see Judith 15:9-10). Fruit of the mystery: *perseverance.*

FAVORITE CATHOLIC PRAYERS

Note: The Apostles' Creed, Our Father, Hail Mary, Glory Be, and Hail Holy Queen can be found in Appendix I.

Morning Offering

O Jesus, through the Immaculate Heart of Mary, I offer thee all my prayers, works, joys, and sufferings of this day, in union with the Holy Sacrifice of the Mass throughout the world, in reparation for my sins, for all the intentions of thy Sacred Heart, and for all the intentions of the Holy Father for this month. Amen.

Guardian Angel Prayer

Angel of God, my guardian dear, to whom God's love commits me here: Ever this day be at my side, to light and guard, to rule and guide. Amen.

Angelus

(This prayer is to be prayed at noon daily. It may also be prayed in the early morning and in the evening.)

Leader: The angel of the Lord declared unto Mary,
Response: And she conceived of the Holy Spirit.

All: Hail Mary. . . .

Leader: Behold the handmaiden of the Lord.
Response: Let it be done unto me according to thy word.
All: Hail Mary. . . .
Leader: (all bow their heads) And the Word became flesh,
Response: And dwelt among us.
All: Hail Mary. . . .

Leader: Pray for us, O holy Mother of God,
Response: That we may be made worthy of the promises of Christ.

Leader: Let us pray.
All: Pour forth, we beseech thee, O Lord, thy grace into our hearts: that we, to whom the incarnation of Christ, thy Son, was made known by the message of an angel, may by his passion and cross be brought to the glory of his resurrection. Through the same Christ our Lord. Amen.

Prayer to St. Michael the Archangel

St. Michael, the Archangel, defend us in battle. Be our protection against the wickedness and snares of the devil. May God rebuke him, we humbly pray; and do thou, O prince of the heavenly host, by the power of God, thrust into hell Satan and the other evil spirits, who wander the world seeking the ruin of souls. Amen.

Memorare of St. Bernard

Remember, O most gracious Virgin Mary, that never was it known that anyone who fled to thy protection, implored thy help, or sought thy intercession, was left unaided. Inspired by this confidence, I fly unto thee, O Virgin of virgins, my mother. To thee I come, before thee I stand, sinful and sorrowful. O Mother of the Word Incarnate, despise not my petitions, but in thy mercy, hear and answer me. Amen.

Novena Prayer to St. Thérèse of the Child Jesus ("The Little Flower")

(This prayer should be said for nine consecutive days. Say the prayer, mention your petition, and then say five Our Fathers, five Hail Marys, and five Glory Be prayers. On the ninth day, say these prayers ten times in thankful anticipation.)

St. Thérèse, the Little Flower, please pick me a rose from the heavenly garden and send it to me with a message of love. Ask God to grant me the favor I thee implore, and tell him I'll love him each day more and more.

Act of Contrition

(Say this prayer each night before bed, after an examination of conscience of your day.)

O my God, I am sorry for my sins with all my heart. In choosing to do wrong and failing to do good, I have sinned against you whom I should love above all things. I firmly intend, with the help of your grace, to confess my sins, to do penance, to sin no more, and to avoid the near occasion of sin. Our Savior Jesus Christ suffered and died for us. In His name, my God, have mercy. Amen.

The following two meditations are beautiful prayers to say as you consecrate your home and your family to the patronage of the Sacred Heart of Jesus and the Immaculate Heart of Mary.

Consecration to the Sacred Heart of Jesus

O Sacred Heart of Jesus, filled with infinite love, broken by my ingratitude and pierced by my sins and yet loving me still, accept the consecration that I make to thee of all that I am and all that I have. Take every faculty of my soul and body, and draw me day by day nearer and nearer to thy sacred side, and there, as I can bear the lesson, teach me thy blessed ways.

O Sacred Heart of Jesus, once in agony, have pity on the dying. Amen.

Consecration to the Immaculate Heart of Mary

O Mary, my Mother, I consecrate myself to your Immaculate Heart. I am all yours and all I have is yours. Keep me under your mantle of mercy, protect me as your child, and lead my soul safely to Jesus in heaven. Purify all that I give you and give it to Jesus, that he may use it to help save the world and souls. Amen.

Spiritual Communion

(This prayer is to be said as you pass a Catholic church, or anytime, especially on days when you cannot attend Mass.)

O Jesus, I turn toward the holy tabernacle where you live hidden for the love of me. I love you, O my God. I cannot receive you in Holy Communion. Come nevertheless and visit me with your grace. Come spiritually into my heart. Purify it. Sanctify it. Render it like unto your own. Amen.

Chaplet of Divine Mercy

(This prayer can be said using rosary beads.)

1. Begin with:
   One Our Father
   One Hail Mary
   The Apostles' Creed

2. On the "Our Father" beads say:
   "Eternal Father, I offer thee the Body and Blood, Soul and Divinity of your dearly beloved Son, our Lord Jesus Christ, in atonement for our sins and those of the whole world."

3. On the "Hail Mary" beads say:
   "For the sake of his sorrowful Passion, have mercy on us and on the whole world."

4. In conclusion, repeat three times:
   "Holy God, Holy Mighty One, Holy Immortal One, have mercy on us and on the whole world."

Young Children's Thanksgiving Prayer

Thank you for the world so sweet.
Thank you for the food we eat.
Thank you for the birds that sing.
Thank you, God, for everything! Amen.

Children's Prayer to the Sacred Heart of Jesus

Most Sacred Heart of Jesus, have mercy on us.
Sweet Heart of Jesus, I put my trust in you.

Children's Prayer to the Immaculate Heart of Mary

Most Pure Heart of Mary, keep my heart free from sin.
Sweet Heart of Mary, be my salvation.

Simple Children's Prayer Before Communion

My Jesus, I need you. It's hard for me to be good.
Come to make my soul strong.
Give my soul its Food and Drink.
Let me grow in love for you. Amen.

Simple Children's Prayer After Communion

My Jesus, I love you. Thank you for coming to me.
Stay with me always. I need your help to be good.
Help me to be more like you. Amen.

Prayer to St. Anne (a mother's prayer)

St. Anne, my dear mother and most compassionate protectress, receive graciously my poor efforts to do you honor. May I ever be devoted to you with a heart full of childlike humility and submission. May your example encourage me, your intercession strengthen me, your goodness console me! Permit me with all my heart to commend you to my children, as you consecrated Mary, your child of grace, entirely to God. I beg you to obtain for me the grace to train my children for him, and with them to labor perseveringly for heaven. As you lived in holy harmony with St. Joachim, so may love, union, devotion, and the zeal for virtue reign in my household, that we may belong to that host of blessed spouses who with you will love, praise, and glorify the Most High forever and ever. Amen.

Prayer to St. Joseph (a father's prayer)

(Reprinted with the permission of FAMILIA, 3205 Roosevelt St. NE, Minneapolis, MN 55418.)

Glorious St. Joseph, guide and protector of the Holy Family,
We ask that you obtain for us from your Son, Jesus,
the strength and wisdom to lead our families
to their Father in heaven.
Most chaste spouse of the Blessed Virgin Mary,
may we imitate your obedience to the will of God
and be ever mindful of the vocation
to which we have been called. Amen.

appendix III

POPULAR CATHOLIC SAINTS

Saints for Children

St. Sebastian

January 20 — Martyr, Patron of Athletes

The son of wealthy parents, Sebastian became the captain of the Roman guards protecting the emperor. He was accused of following Jesus and was persecuted. Before the emperor had him killed, he healed and tended to the needs of many prisoners.

St. Agnes

January 21 — Virgin, Martyr, Patroness of Young Girls

As a beautiful young girl, Agnes refused to be married, instead choosing Jesus as her spouse. She was persecuted, yet she still praised Jesus. She died making the Sign of the Cross. This gentle saint's name means *lamb*.

St. Dominic Savio

March 9 — Patron of Children

An Italian boy who at age 5 became an altar boy, Dominic told St. John Bosco that he wanted to be a priest. He studied hard and loved to pray. His schoolmates liked his kindness and cheerfulness. As he was ill and lay dying, he said, "What beautiful things I see!"

St. Patrick

March 17 — Bishop, Patron of Ireland

Patrick converted pagan Ireland to Christianity by using the abundant three-leaf clover (shamrock) of Ireland to explain the Holy Trinity.

St. Joseph

March 19 — Foster-father of Jesus and Husband of Mary; Patron of Fathers, the Universal Church, and the Dying

Joseph was the loving spouse of the Blessed Virgin Mary and the earthly father of Jesus.

St. Joan of Arc

May 30 — Virgin, Martyr, Patroness of Soldiers

A young peasant girl with pious parents, she had a special devotion to St. Michael the Archangel. She led a small army under the banner of Jesus and Mary to conquer her country's enemies.

St. Aloysius Gonzaga

June 21 — Religious, Patron of Youths

A young prince who gave up all to follow Jesus, Aloysius became a Jesuit novice and nursed the victims of an epidemic in Rome. Before reaching the priesthood, he died from illness while gazing at a crucifix.

St. Maria Goretti

July 6 — Virgin, Martyr, Model of Purity

Maria was an obedient and happy Italian farm girl who was attacked by an evil boy. She resisted his evil, then forgave him and prayed for his repentance before she died. After prison, the evil boy sought forgiveness and became a Capuchin lay brother.

St. Clare

August 11 — Virgin, Patroness of Television, Foundress of the Poor Clares

As a young girl from a noble family, Clare gave herself to Jesus and lived a life of poverty, prayer, and fasting. She worked with St. Francis of Assisi and was devoted to the Blessed Sacrament.

St. Francis of Assisi

October 4 — Patron of Catholic Action, Founder of the Franciscans

He left his wealthy family to devote his life to Jesus and lived in poverty as a missionary preaching repentance, faith, and peace with all people. He had the stigmata, bearing the five wounds of Christ. He's also known as the protector of animals.

Saints for Parents

St. Joseph

March 19 — Foster-father of Jesus and Husband of Mary; Patron of Fathers, the Universal Church, and the Dying

A lowly carpenter of the house of David, Joseph was the chaste spouse of the Blessed Virgin Mary. He was a "just man" chosen by God to be the protector of Jesus. He is a father's model for charity, chastity, and fortitude.

St. Anthony of Padua

June 13 — Priest, Doctor of the Church, Patron of the Poor and Lost Articles

Anthony was a Franciscan missionary who converted thousands as a preacher and "wonder-worker." His tongue is still incorrupt (not deteriorated). His relics are cherished, and his reputation for miracles is worldwide.

St. Anne

July 26 — Mother of Mary, Patroness of Housewives

Her name means *grace*. She was the mother of the Blessed Virgin Mary and grandmother of Jesus. There is the story that she and her husband, Joachim, had been without children until an angel said they would have a daughter who would be honored by the entire world. She is a mother's model of love and faith.

St. Joachim

July 26 — Father of Mary

There is the tradition that Joachim was of the tribe of Judah and the house of David, and that he lived in Nazareth. He fasted and prayed for forty days in the desert to have children. An angel appeared to him and said that his prayers would be answered. He is a model for husbands and fathers.

St. Maximilian Kolbe

August 14 — Priest, Martyr, Founder of the Knights of the Immaculate

A Franciscan who was ill most of his life, Maximilian was devoted to the Blessed Virgin and used modern technology to reach millions. He died a martyr in Auschwitz, the Nazi death camp.

St. Monica

August 27 — Patroness of Mothers
She was the mother of St. Augustine. During great trials, she prayed fervently for the conversion of her son, which was granted. Mothers have implored her help in times of distress.

St. Thérèse of the Child Jesus ("The Little Flower")

October 1 — Virgin, Doctor of the Church, Patroness of Missions
As a child, Thérèse was cured by the Blessed Virgin. As a Carmelite nun, she offered all her little sacrifices to help priests save souls. She is a highly favored saint and is always pictured with beautiful roses.

St. Jude

October 28 — Apostle, Martyr, Patron of Impossible Cases
Jude was the cousin of Jesus. According to tradition, Jude was a missionary with St. Simon in Persia, where they preached and healed, making many converts. His relics are honored in St. Peter's Basilica in Rome.

appendix IV

MEDIA RESOURCES

Books

Here are some great books for children that you can find at your local Catholic bookstore.

Bible Story Library (excellent, with simple rhyming and pictures; Arch Books)

The Caterpillar That Came to Church by Irene J. Hooker, Susan Andrews Brindle, and Miriam Andrews Lademan (Our Sunday Visitor)

The Children's Book of Saints by Louis M. Savary (Regina Press)

Dear God by M. Rogers (Brimax Books)

God Bless by M. Rogers (Brimax Books)

God Made Me (C.R. Gibson)

Great Men: New Testament by Rev. Jude Winkler, O.F.M. Conv. (Catholic Book Publishing)

Great Men: Old Testament by Rev. Jude Winkler, O.F.M. Conv. (Catholic Book Publishing)

Great Women of the Bible by Rev. Jude Winkler, O.F.M. Conv. (Catholic Book Publishing)

A Little Book of Poems and Prayers by Joan Walsh Anglund (Simon & Schuster)

My First Picture Bible Stories, Catholic Edition by Kenneth N. Taylor (Our Sunday Visitor)

My Little Book of Prayers illustrated by Kathy Allert (Western Publishing)

Our Friends the Saints by George Brundage (Catholic Book Publishing)

Poems and Prayers for the Very Young by Martha Alexander (Random House)

Videotapes

CCC of America

Bernadette: The Princess of Lourdes
The Day the Sun Danced: The True Story of Fatima
Francis: The Knight of Assisi
Juan Diego: Messenger of Guadalupe
Patrick: Brave Shepherd of the Emerald Isle
and many more!

Our Sunday Visitor

"Stories and Parables" video series, which includes *The Wondering Kitten and The Lost Sheep, Sammy's Friends and The Sower and The Seed, The Great Feast and Come to the Wedding Feast, A Squirrel's Tale and The Foolish Rich Man,* and *The Elephant's Picnic and The Place of Honor.*

A Walk Through the Mass with Bishop Donald W. Wuerl

Hanna–Barbera Productions

"The Greatest Adventure: Stores from the Bible" series, which includes, *Samson and Delilah, Daniel and the Lions' Den, Joshua and the Battle of Jericho, David and Goliath, Noah's Ark, Moses, The Nativity,* and *The Easter Story.*

Big Idea Company

"Veggie Tales" series

Audiotapes

Our Sunday Visitor

The Rosary on Tape by Msgr. Owen F. Campion
The Mysteries of the Rosary by Bishop Donald W. Wuerl
Stations of the Cross and the Gospel of the Passion by Msgr. Owen F. Campion

ABOUT THE AUTHORS

Kathy Pierce, a native of Oklahoma City, holds a bachelor's degree in advertising and a master's degree in gerontology. She worked briefly designing and selling advertising, and for six years as the director of marketing for a large nursing home organization. She and her husband, Larry, reside in Edmond, Oklahoma, with their six children, all of whom have received home-schooling.

Lori Rowland, also a native of Oklahoma City, has a bachelor's degree in journalism. She worked as a public relations and advertising coordinator for a health care system, and as a co-ordinator for provider relations for the same enterprise. She and her husband, Paul, live in Jacksonville, Florida, with their four children. Lori is very active at the parochial school that her three oldest children attend.

Our Sunday Visitor's
BIG BOOK of Ideas
for Children's Faith Formation

Easy – Energizing
Effective – NEW

Easy to use with any curriculum, educational materials, or alone. Included materials lists, reproducible patterns, illustrations, and easy-to-follow directions make this resource user-friendly. A comprehensive topic index makes what you are looking for easy to find.

Energizing because teachers and children are fueled with interactive activities, crafts, rhymes, games, and easy-to-sing songs. Quick to prepare and fun to use, there is a multitude of options for various ages, class sizes, and learning styles.

Effective for children and teachers because children learn best when they are able to actively respond. Each idea offers an encounter with faith that children can apply to their lives and won't forget.

The Big Book of Ideas for Children's Faith Formation
Edited by Beth Branigan McNamara
with Gina Wright McKeever and Sue Robinson
0-87973-018-8, paper, 352 pp., **$24.95**

Available at bookstores. MasterCard, VISA, and Discover customers can order direct from **Our Sunday Visitor** by calling **1-800-348-2440**. Order online at www.osv.com. Or, send payment **plus** $5.95 shipping/handling fee per order to:

Our Sunday Visitor
200 Noll Plaza • Huntington, IN 46750
1-800-348-2440 • e-mail: osvbooks@osv.com

OurSundayVisitor

• Periodicals • Books • Tapes • Curricula • Software • Offering Envelopes • For a free catalog call 1-800-348-2440

Our Sunday Visitor . . .
Your Source for Discovering the Riches of the Catholic Faith

Our Sunday Visitor has an extensive line of materials for young children, teens, and adults. Our books, Bibles, booklets, CD-ROMs, audios, and videos are available in bookstores worldwide.

To receive a FREE full-line catalog or for more information, call **Our Sunday Visitor** at **1-800-348-2440**. Or write, **Our Sunday Visitor** / 200 Noll Plaza / Huntington, IN 46750.

- -

Please send me: ___A catalog
Please send me materials on:
___Apologetics and catechetics   ___Reference works
___Prayer books   ___Heritage and the saints
___The family   ___The parish
Name_____
Address_____Apt._____
City_____State_____Zip_____
Telephone (   ) _____

A19BBABP

- -

Please send a friend: ___A catalog
Please send a friend materials on:
____Apologetics and catechetics   ____Reference works
____Prayer books   ____Heritage and the saints
____The family   ____The parish
Name_____
Address_____Apt._____
City_____State_____Zip_____
Telephone (   ) _____

A19BBABP

- -

Our Sunday Visitor
200 Noll Plaza
Huntington, IN 46750
Toll free: **1-800-348-2440**
E-mail: osvbooks@osv.com
Website: www.osv.com